POWERFUL WEAPONS OF SPIRITUAL WARFARE

FREEDOM
From
OPPRESSIONS

POWERFUL WEAPONS OF SPIRITUAL WARFARE

FREEDOM
From
OPPRESSIONS

Roger D. Muñoz

POWERFUL WEAPONS OF SPIRITUAL WARFARE

FREEDOM
From
OPPRESSIONS

Roger D. Muñoz

CHRIST DELIVERANCE
MINISTRY OF DELIVERANCE AND HEALING
Seattle WA 98115
www.cristolibera.org

Copyright © 2015 by Roger DeJesus Munoz Caballero

All rights reserved. No portion of this book may be reproduced, stored in a retrieval system, or transmitted in any form or by any means, mechanical, electronic, photocopying, recording, or otherwise, without written permission from the publisher.

Published by:
CHRIST LIBERA
MINISTRY OF DELIVERANCE AND HEALING
Seattle WA 98115

www.cristolibera.org

Printed and bound in the USA

ISBN-13:978-0-9964859-3-7
ISBN-10:0996485937

Roger Muñoz is a servant of God who trained me in the ministry of deliverance long ago and also had the blessing of traveling to USA for further training in the deliverance ministry. Thanks to Jesus Christ that through His servant, I am now minister deliverance and many have been free in this beautiful country of Japan.

— Pastor James Teruya
Renacier Christian Church In Japan

Pastor Roger D Muñoz is leaving a legacy for those who want to learn more about the ministry of deliverance. This book is an excellent tool for all ministers of the Kingdom of God and His righteousness. Acknowledge the hard work in deliverance ministry that God has given him.

— Pastor Eugenio Manuel Torres
Our Reformed Church Christ Justice
Santa Marta, Colombia, South America

The Servant Roger Muñoz has been repeatedly invited as panel conference aired on themes of deliverance and spiritual warfare which has been a blessing.

— Pastor Jose Ramos
Driver Radio Program Pastors United For Christ
President Of Hispanic Evangelical Alliance North

Roger Muñoz has been a great blessing to my life and my ministry, because through his life and ministry of deliverance, we were able to provide better service to God and His Church, bringing freedom to those who once were held captive by Satan. May the Lord bless you and continue saving and prosper you in everything you do.

— Apostol Mario Bonillas
Ebenezer Church Council Founder USA.

Roger Muñoz is one of our volunteers to the Ministry of Immigration Detention in the Northwest Detention Center in Tacoma Washington, USA, once a month preaching the gospel and has led many people to Christ.

—Pastor Habtom Ghebru

Roger Muñoz used to be a businessman in the country of Colombia in South America, but from the moment of his conversion to Jesus Christ, there was born a passion to free those who are captive and under the oppression of evil spirits. He is the founder of the ministry "Christ Libera". Many are those who have benefited from their service delivery in the United States and elsewhere.

— Rev. Jorge Gutierrez
Christian Church Of The Americas
Seattle Washington USA.

TABLE OF CONTENTS

AUTHOR 11
GRATITUDE 12
PURPOSE 13
INTRODUCTION 14
1. AUTHOR'S TESTIMONY 17
2. FIVE REASONS WHY THIS BOOK WAS WRITTEN 23
3. TEN BIBLICAL REASONS 25
4. TEN KEY REQUIREMENTS TO BE FREED 29
5. KEY FOR DELIVERANCE 33
6. THE PROBLEM AND SOLUTION TO SIN AND CURSES 35
7. CONFERENCE OF DELIVERANCE 47
8. DELIVERANCE IN A CONFERENCE 61
9. GENERAL DOORWAYS OF DEMONIC ENTRANCES 67
10. CONFERENCE ABOUT THE DOORWAYS 75
11. CREATION OF A DELIVERANCE TEAM 115
12. HOW TO DESTROY THE MOST COMMON WITCHCRAFT 153
13. TESTIMONIES AND PROCESS OF DELIVERANCE 161
14. FORMULARY QUESTIONS 191

AUTHOR

Roger D Muñoz, a married man and with two beautiful children, is the man God chose to found and guide the Christ Deliverance, a ministry of Deliverance and Healing, with its headquarters in Seattle, Washington, in the United States.

In addition to serving locally, the ministry serves in all the states of USA and the rest of the world where God chooses, where there is need for service delivery to Internet technology, phones, digital cameras, translators and sometimes traveling to where God sends him. This Ministry has performed thousands of deliverance, most of them are on its website www.cristolibera.org and its YouTube channel.

Roger is a volunteer preacher in the Ministry of Immigration Detention in the Northwest Detention Center in Tacoma Washington, USA.

He has been repeatedly invited as a member of the aired Conference Panel on issues of deliverance and spiritual warfare, in the Radio Program "Pastors United for Christ Evangelical Hispanic Alliance Northwest."

He has given many seminars, conferences, workshops and has trained pastors and leaders who are already ministering deliverance to their congregations.

GRATITUDE

I'm very grateful to Jesus Christ for having me redeemed and rescued through the precious blood he shed on the Calvary's Cross, and by having me as a useful instrument, so HE can manifest and bring me wisdom to write this book.

I thank God for having me brought to my pastors; Jorge y Felisa Gutiérrez, they were my spiritual guides since the very beginning here in the Earth, and I also thank God for teaching me to be Bible-centric and Christ-centric.

I thank my beloved wife as well, Gladys, for all her patience, compression and support to be with me in every moment, and equally to my beloved sons, Roger y Nestor Muñoz. To my lovely mother Isabel Caballero for being always with me. To Juanita Álvarez, Mirella Thomas, Franklin Bulmez, Emerson Mauricio Cortes, Vanessa de la Cerda, Rudy Américo Fernández, Ana Julia Dulcey, Cristian Santana Monterroza, to Carmen Kucinski for their greater love and effort in editing this book, to Alex Godefroy for his tremendous and invaluable help in the cover design and in almost every aspect of this book, this son of God helped us more than we expected.

Moreover, I thank those who believe in this minister in one way or another, from which this book is the product.

PURPOSE

That every Christian ministry, leader, church, cell, group and meetings in all parts of the world, including countries, cities, towns, and houses have this book in their hands. That they study and put into practice this simple and effective method of deliverance from demons and sickness so that they may be free, healed, and able to remain safe from demons and sickness. You can practice this by yourself (self-deliverance) or as recommended: with a Christian, who is mature in its faith.

INTRODUCTION

Welcome and congratulation! The heart of God is very glad for what you are about to discover, learn and put into practice for you own freedom and health. Your heart will be very happy for you, your family, and the kingdom of God; because Jesus Christ achieved a complete and total victory at the Calvary's Cross shedding his precious Blood, freeing us from the sins, Curses, iniquities and demonic agreements with their respective destruction.

This Manual was developed because of the need to form and sentences in a letter, which will facilitate printing and copying for use. It was mainly developed to facilitate the work of those that will be involved in deliverance and ministries of deliverance. It is highly recommended that you purchase: Freedom from The Oppressions, which is the base of this Manual. And this Manual is very important for all of our Freedom books Series.

The majority of Christians are being tormented by demons with diseases, and they do not notice that; so they accept the diseases as if our Lord Jesus would not have carried them to the Cross.

> *You will know the tools that will keep you healthy and free of demons.*

You will learn which are the

causes or doors of entrances to that disease or misery, pain, and sadness... Moreover, you will be able to be free of that torment. Furthermore, you will learn how to be free from sexual thoughts that are tormenting you. You will also learn how to create teams of deliverances in your church to do more powerful prayers of freedom; overthrowing demonic structures of wickedness, you will know how you, or with the help of another Christian, can be free of witchcraft, pains, diseases, demons and much more, how to keep you in complete freedom and health for the glory and honor of Our Lord and Savior Jesus!

Finally, you will find testimonies of deliverance with their processes that you can use, AMEN!

Ah! I recommend you to read these Books several times!

1.
AUTHOR'S TESTIMONY

I was looking for help," for someone who could pray for me and at the same time deliver me from the continuous demonic attacks and oppressions I was receiving. I did not find it! I could not make it! However, some people who believe in Jesus Christ came to me. They thought they could help me, and for that reason I asked them for help, I asked them if they could pray for me to deliver me from the demonic attacks and oppressions I was receiving. Even though they tried, they could not do it! My incertitude was growing more and more, and I questioned myself: Is there anyone who can do it? Where is that person who can help me?

Well... Everything started around the 90's. Back then I didn't know the LORD JESUS CHRIST like I know him now, and I know I will be discovering more about him... like most of believers say: "I wasn't able to convert in the faith toward our LORD".

The symptoms of the attacks and oppressions kept going more and more, which I started to feel several times when I went to bed, and I felt it got out of my body and began to fly. On another occasion, my body was paralyzed. I felt an intense oppression that prevented me from moving. I did not know what to do! I was terrified! Sometimes I felt someone next to me on the bed, and that happened night after night.

I had many dreams that felt real, in which I had sex with unknown women. They seemed to be so real that when I saw their faces they were very beautiful, good-looking women, but when I saw them with focus I noticed their faces changed. They had skull faces! Moreover, for that reason, I had many nightmares.

The irony was that no one knew about this, I did not talk about it, and so I was getting used to that lifestyle. For a long time, I read the Bible to feel better... specially the **_Psalm 91_**; I remember I slept with a Bible in my hands! On other occasions, I left the book opened in the same psalms. Moreover, I kept doing that for many years! I was used to that lifestyle, an ordinary life apparently.

> *Is there anyone who can make it? Where is that person that can help me?*

1.1. JESUS CHRIST's Manifestation

In the year 2002 I went to the United States of North America (USA), where I live at this moment. Three months later, when I was relaxing around 3:00 p.m., I had my eyes closed, but consciously awake, "I felt a presence in my bedroom". Which got my attention right away. When I opened my eyes, *"I saw a human figure"* It was white and shining! From the figure light rays came out, I saw it! I could not see its face! It was very strong, I was scared, so I closed my eyes, and then I felt he came closer, he took the bed sheet and covered me with it. *"I was not expecting that, then I felt the presence was not there anymore, I opened my eyes, and he was not there!"* Everything went normal, I have not forgotten that figure I saw, it was our LORD manifesting to me... What an honor and privilege! I called my mother immediately by phone, and I said to her after the supernatural encounter: Mother I saw God! However, my life went on as usual apparently, with sins, and the demonic attacks and oppressions kept going.

The next year, after that supernatural experience from our LORD JESUS CHRIST, I had another supernatural experience that affected my life deeply, in one way that God only knows how to do it. That experience brought me to my senses, and I started to meditate about my life. Moreover, it was with the help of the HOLY SPIRIT was bringing testimony and conviction of sin; I realized that something was very wrong with me, so I recognized my weak ness and sin condition.

Moreover, I couldn't do anything with my strength. This was when I gave everything I had to my Lord JESUS CHRIST. Since then everything changed. My life started to be different and the Holy Spirit guided me, I found the Christian Church of the America with Jorge Gutiérrez, my current pastor, to know more about God and his ways, that was the right place for that purpose.

However, the demonic attacks kept going; I did not understand why. If I gave my whole being to Jesus Christ, how could the attacks go on?

However, what I did not know was that God was in control. He allowed it and for that reason he introduces me in the area of deliverance. Thereby, he started to train me and qualify me using the retreats and encounters that took place at the Church. He used me in the deliverance, and he surprised me.

Despite all that, the demonic attacks kept going, but I was introduced to the presence and the ways of God gradually and obeying his word and command. Moreover, that was how the attacks and oppressions were decreasing.

1.2. Auto-deliverance from Demonic Oppressions

On June 2011, the LORD JESUS CHRIST had something big and great for my life. He changed my job and put me in a new one. Which I did not imagine I would EVER get! He chose me to be part of his work team, his kingdom, and his concerns in the earth, and, of course, with the greatest of the bosses, THE LORD as my great chief. What a great privilege to be chosen by Him, and for his grace, I started to work full-time in the area of Deliverance and Health.

In this Ministry, I began doing auto-deliverances on myself, being free in many areas. With the authority that only Jesus provides, the demons started to get out of my body, God had a traced purpose which it would develop without any obstacle because he used and kept using my experience in deliverance and auto-deliverance for the body of Christ.

Jesus Christ had liberated me from what I wasn't totally free before! They are gone! They escaped!

I help thousands of people around the entire world, from all countries and different nationalities. Setting them free of boundages and demonic oppressions. Using digital cameras through internet, phones or meeting them personally: face to face.

After all these battles and auto-deliverances, I can say Jesus Christ had delivered me from what I was not totally free before! They are gone! They escaped! All those attacks that existed for years and all those fights, battles, and demonic oppressions; they were gone... That is how this Ministry of Deliverance and Health was created; Christ deliverances.

1.3. Serving JESUS CHRIST

Therefore, dear reader, the demon world is real, it exists, and there isn't much information about this matter. Today, Churches with this kind of Ministry of Deliverance and Health are not recognized. That is why I'm compromised full time to the LORD JESUS CHRIST and with his church to support the people of God with the gift he has given to me through the Holy Spirit.

You can see, Brother or Sister, that with Christ I have many reasons and experiences that I can talk about or mention in detail. There isn't much information or help on this matter. Neither has the Ministry of Deliverance and Healing that the Lord himself has delegated to his Church to set his people free and enjoy a supernatural relationship with Him.

2.
FIVE REASONS WHY THIS BOOK WAS WRITTEN

I. The majority of Christians are bound and sick because of the enemy, and they do not know or understand how to be freed and healed.

II. All Christians should know how to be free and how to put this information into practice.

III. The majority of Christian churches do not have anyone, not even the pastor that knows how to do deliverance or heal their members.

IV. Churches need deliverance teams, and this book explains how to create them.

V. Many people do not know how to use the Internet or computers and don't have smartphones where they can search for help. Many faraway places do not have the technology or Internet. they are in need of a physical book that can be found in various languages.

The majority of this information comes from years of experience and study. Please, allow the Holy Spirit to guide you and confirm the truth in your life. This book is practical and does not leave much room for interpretation. It was created to be as simple and straightforward as possible.

> *All Christians should know how to be free and how to put this information into practice.*

3.
TEN BIBLICAL REASONS

In this section, we demonstrate by the light of the Word why we do deliverance and how we do it.

1. It was Jesus who gave us the power and authority.

    Luke 9:1-2 *"Then he called his twelve disciples together, and gave them power and authority over all devils, and to cure diseases. 2 And he sent them to preach the kingdom of God, and to heal the sick."*

2. Casting out demons is part of our mission and goal. They hold us to ourselves. We must remember that, what is more, important is Salvation; that our names are written in heaven.

    Luke 10:20 *"Notwithstanding in this rejoice not, that the spirits are subject unto you, but rather rejoice, because your names are written in heaven."*

3. The apostles continued doing the work that Jesus had taught them. We should also do the same. It is one of our primary purposes, and who ever is reading this book of deliverance will do it.

Acts 5:16 *"After this I will return, and will build again the tabernacle of David, which is fallen down; and I will build again the ruins thereof, and I will set it up:"*

4. We do not free ourselves, we are the medium, the instrument through which Christ frees us through the Power of the Holy Spirit. We give Him all of the glory forever.

Romans 15:18-19ᵃ *" For I will not dare to speak of any of those things which Christ hath not wrought by me, to make the Gentiles obedient, by word and deed,¹⁹ Through mighty signs and wonders, by the power of the Spirit of God;"*

> **Christ frees us through the Power of the Holy Spirit**

5. There is a lot of information in the Bible about people who have been set free. Jesus did it. He is our model.

Mark 9:21 *"And he asked his father, how long is it ago since this came unto him? Moreover, he said, Of a child."*

6. All demons can be immediately cast out in the Name of Jesus, but sometimes they do not want to leave and we must ask them why; what legal right do they believe they have, what to call them, how many there are, etc. so that we can cast them out.

Mark 5:6-10 *"But when he saw Jesus afar off, he ran and worshipped him,7 And cried with a loud voice, and said, What have I to do with thee, Jesus, thou Son of the most high God? I adjure thee by God that thou torment me not.⁸ For he said unto him, Come out of the man, thou unclean spirit.⁹ And he asked him, What is thy name? Moreover, he answered, saying, My name is*

Legion: for we are many. ¹⁰ And he besought him much that he would not send them away out of the country.

7. The majority of sickness is caused by sin, through the disobedience to God.

   John 5:14 *"¹⁴ Afterward Jesus findeth him in the temple, and said unto him, Behold, thou art made whole: sin no more, lest a worse thing come unto thee."*

8. It is very rare that a person only has one demon. Generally, there are various demons and one leader whom you must carefully search for, and they will guide you how to cast out the rest.

   Mark 5:9 *And he asked him, What is thy name? And he answered, saying, My name is Legion: for we are many.*

9. Christians can have demons, and they are the only ones who can be set free. Everyone we have served in our ministry is a Christian. A non-Christian, one who has not accepted Christ as his Savior, does not have the faith to be set free. Deliverance is for the children of God. "The bread is for the children."

   Matthew 15:21-28

   ²¹ Then Jesus went thence, and departed into the coasts of Tyre and Sidon. 22 And, behold, a woman of Canaan came out of the same coasts, and cried unto him, saying, Have mercy on me, O Lord, thou son of David; my daughter is grievously vexed with a devil. 23 But he answered her not a word. And his disciples came and besought him, saying, Send her away; for she crieth after us. 24 But he answered and said, I am not sent but unto the lost sheep of the house of Israel. 25 Then came she and worshipped him, saying, Lord, help me. 26 But he answered and said, It is not meet to take the children's bread, and to cast it to dogs. 27 And she said, Truth, Lord: yet the dogs eat of the crumbs which fall from their masters' table. 28 Then Jesus answered and said unto her, O woman, great is thy faith: be it unto thee even as thou wilt. And her daughter was made whole from that very hour.

10. We should confess our sins in order to be forgiven and healed. This is what the questionnaire talks about.

    James 5:16 *Confess your faults one to another, and pray one for another, that ye may be healed. The effectual fervent prayer of a righteous man availeth muh.*

THIS IS THE PURPOSE OF THE QUESTIONARE YOU FIND HERE

4.
TEN KEY REQUIREMENTS TO BE FREED

I. Accept Christ. Deliverance is for those who confess Jesus as Lord and Savior; it is for Christians.

II. Seek help. This is a test of you wanting to be free, when you take the initiative to seek help.

III. Believe that you will be freed. You must believe, there are many who doubt.

IV. Have an intense desire for deliverance. Many do not want to be free.

V. Fill in the Deliverance Form. These questions are made to look for possible doorways for demons.

VI. Follow the recommended steps. Trust what is written here and what is explained to you.

VII. Do not be contentious. There are many who want to know more than others.

VIII. Confess and renounce your sins. Without this, there is no deliverance.

IX. Believe that a Christian can have demons. If you do not believe, you cannot be free.

X. You should not be practicing sins. This is one of the reasons why someone can not be free. The devil has a legal right to be in a man that practices sin

Deliverance is for the children of God.

Mark 7:27 (KJV)

²⁷ But Jesus said unto her, let the children first be filled: for it is not meet to take the children's bread, and to cast it unto the dogs.

> ***Deliverance is for the children of God.***

Important!

If you have not accepted Jesus as your Lord and Savior and want to do it now, please repeat this prayer:

> *"Lord Jesus, you are the Son of God who came to die for my sins on the Cross of Calvary, now I accept you as my Savior and Lord, forgive my sins, I accept your forgiveness, write my name in the Book of Life. Holy Spirit comes into my heart, my life and dwell with me. Thank you Jesus, today I consecrate my life to Thee. Thank you, in the name of the Father of the Son and of the Holy Spirit, Amen."*

> *Fill in the Deliverance Form. These questions are made to look for possible doorways for demons.*

5.
KEY FOR DELIVERANCE

Passage of confession, repentance, resignation, forgiveness, and acceptance.

This step is crucial because it is the key to your deliverance. After filling out your form, calmly take each point of it and confess it, renounce and ask Jesus to forgive you if this is the case.

Example: My Lord Jesus, I confess the sin of pornography, I repent and renounce this sin and ask you to forgive me in the name of Jesus. Thank you for forgiving me. I reject Demons of pornography and the like of them, I do not want them, I do not accept them, I reject them in the Name of Jesus, So OUT, OUT, OUT IN THE NAME OF JESUS!

Do this for all the sins. The more you confess your sins and renounce the devil, the more you will feel free, and feel lighter.

Important note. If you are conducting personal deliverance, after asking and receiving forgiveness, start casting out demons in Jesus' name immediately and be persistent on this. But if you are conducting deliverance for someone else, first wait for the person to confess his sins and ask for forgiveness for all points. This is in order for you to focus solely on casting out the demons. As no demon will have a legal right anymore.

> *After filling out your form, calmly take each point of it and confess it, renounce and ask Jesus to forgive you if it is the case.*

6.
THE PROBLEM AND SOLUTION TO SIN AND CURSES

6.1. Origin.

Curses have existed since the beginning of creation since Adam and Eve sinned. Remember that curses are the fruit of sin!

Genesis 3:16-19 Version (KJV)

16 Unto the woman he said, I will greatly multiply thy sorrow and thy conception; in sorrow thou shalt bring forth children; and thy desire shall be to thy husband, and he shall rule over thee.

17 And unto Adam he said, Because thou hast hearkened unto the voice of thy wife, and hast eaten of the tree, of which I commanded thee, saying, Thou shalt not eat of it: Cursed is the ground for thy sake; in sorrow shalt thou eat of it all the days of thy life;

18 Thorns also and thistles shall it bring forth to thee; and thou shalt eat the herb of the field;

19 In the sweat of thy face shalt thou eat bread, till thou return unto the ground; for out of it wast thou taken: for dust thou art, and unto dust shalt thou return.

We can see throughout the Bible that sin brings disaster, ruin, and death, not only to the person who commits the sin, but also to those around it.

If we look at *Deuteronomy 27, 28*, we find a list of disease and disasters that were caused by sin. They were caused by disobeying the Word of God.

The sad part of this is that curses can be passed to your descendants, up to the fourth generation. Although some have lasted up to the tenth. Think about the curses caused by your sins.

Now, today there are many illnesses. Most of which are the consequence of disobedience to the Word of God because of sin. That is the spiritual origin.

In this Ministry of Deliverance, we have seen many people freed from demons that made them sick and were destroying them. They were healed and set free from diabetes, depression, etc.; those things that demons caused by sin.

John 10:10a

The thief cometh not, but for to steal, and to kill, and to destroy

6.2. The Problem.

The world was entirely lost, and all were sinners. We were condemned because the consequence of sin is suffering and death.

Hebrews 9:22 KJV

²² And almost all things are by the law purged with blood; and without shedding of blood is no remission.

Romans 3:23-26

For all have sinned, and come short of the glory of God; ²⁴ Being justified freely by his grace through the redemption that is in Christ Jesus: ²⁵ Whom God hath set forth to be a propitiation through faith in his blood, to declare his righteousness for the remission of sins that are past, through the forbearance of God; ²⁶ To declare, I say, at this time his righteousness: that he might be just, and the justifier of him which believeth in Jesus.

6.3. The Solution.

Jesus Christ is the solution!

John 10:10b KJV

I am come that they might have life, and that they might have it more abundantly.

1 John 3:8b KJV

For this purpose the Son of God was manifested, that he might destroy the works of the devil.

6.3.1. About Curses.

He rescued us from curses and took them all away; those which were passed down through generations and those which were our own. We are no longer guilty for the sins of our ancestors.

Galatians 3:13

¹³ Christ hath redeemed us from the Curse of the law, being made a Curse for us: for it is written, Cursed is every one that hangeth on a tree:

6.3.2. About Sin.

1 John 1:7 King James Version (KJV)

⁷ But if we walk in the light, as he is in the light, we have fellowship one with another, and the blood of Jesus Christ his Son cleanseth us from all sin.

John 1:29 King James Version (KJV)

²⁹ The next day John seeth Jesus coming unto him, and saith, Behold the Lamb of God, which taketh away the sin of the world.

Colossians 2:13-15 King James Version (KJV)

¹³ And you, being dead in your sins and the uncircumcision of your flesh, hath he quickened together with him, having forgiven you all trespasses;

¹⁴ Blotting out the handwriting of ordinances that was against us, which was contrary to us, and took it out of the way, nailing it to his cross;

¹⁵ And having spoiled principalities and powers, he made a shew of them openly, triumphing over them in it.

1 John 2:1-2 King James Version (KJV)

² My little children, these things write I unto you, that ye sin not. And if any man sin, we have an advocate with the Father, Jesus Christ the righteous:

² And he is the propitiation for our sins: and not for ours only, but also for the sins of the whole world.

Revelation 1:5 King James Version (KJV)

⁵ And from Jesus Christ, who is the faithful witness, and the first begotten of the dead, and the prince of the kings of the earth. Unto him that loved us, and washed us from our sins in his own blood,

6.3.3. About Pacts.

Matthew 26:28

For this is my blood of the new testament, which is shed for many for the remission of sins.

6.3.4. About Iniquity.

Titus 2:14 KJV

Who gave himself for us, that he might redeem us from all iniquity, and purify unto himself a peculiar people, zealous of good works.

Isaiah 53:11

¹¹ He shall see of the travail of his soul, and shall be satisfied: by his knowledge shall my righteous servant justify many; for he shall bear their iniquities.

6.3.5. About Sickness and Suffering.

Isaiah 53:3-12 King James Version (KJV)

3 He is despised and rejected of men; a man of sorrows, and acquainted with grief: and we hid as it were our faces from him; he was despised, and we esteemed him not.

4 Surely he hath borne our griefs, and carried our sorrows: yet we did esteem him stricken, smitten of God, and afflicted.

5 But he was wounded for our transgressions, he was bruised for our iniquities: the chastisement of our peace was upon him; and with his stripes we are healed.

6 All we like sheep have gone astray; we have turned every one to his own way; and the Lord hath laid on him the iniquity of us all.

7 He was oppressed, and he was afflicted, yet he opened not his mouth: he is brought as a lamb to the slaughter, and as a sheep before her shearers is dumb, so he openeth not his mouth.

8 He was taken from prison and from judgment: and who shall declare his generation? for he was cut off out of the land of the living: for the transgression of my people was he stricken.

9 And he made his grave with the wicked, and with the rich in his death; because he had done no violence, neither was any deceit in his mouth.

10 Yet it pleased the Lord to bruise him; he hath put him to grief: when thou shalt make his soul an offering for sin, he shall see his seed, he shall prolong his days, and the pleasure of the Lord shall prosper in his hand.

¹¹ He shall see of the travail of his soul, and shall be satisfied: by his knowledge shall my righteous servant justify many; for he shall bear their iniquities.

¹² Therefore will I divide him a portion with the great, and he shall divide the spoil with the strong; because he hath poured out his soul unto death: and he was numbered with the transgressors; and he bare the sin of many, and made intercession for the transgressors.

Isaiah 49:7 King James Version (KJV)

⁷ Thus saith the Lord, the Redeemer of Israel, and his Holy One, to him whom man despiseth, to him whom the nation abhorreth, to a servant of rulers, Kings shall see and arise, princes also shall worship, because of the Lord that is faithful, and the Holy One of Israel, and he shall choose thee.

Isaiah 50:6 King James Version (KJV)

⁶ I gave my back to the smiters, and my cheeks to them that plucked off the hair: I hid not my face from shame and spitting.

Psalm 22:6-8 King James Version (KJV)

⁶ But I am a worm, and no man; a reproach of men, and despised of the people.

⁷ All they that see me laugh me to scorn: they shoot out the lip, they shake the head, saying,

⁸ He trusted on the Lord that he would deliver him: let him deliver him, seeing he delighted in him.

Psalm 69:20 King James Version (KJV)

²⁰ Reproach hath broken my heart; and I am full of heaviness: and I looked for some to take pity, but there was none; and for comforters, but I found none.

Micah 5:1 King James Version (KJV)

⁵ Now gather thyself in troops, O daughter of troops: he hath laid siege against us: they shall smite the judge of Israel with a rod upon the cheek.

Matthew 26:67 King James Version (KJV)

⁶⁷ Then did they spit in his face, and buffeted him; and others smote him with the palms of their hands,

Mark 9:12 King James Version (KJV)

¹² And he answered and told them, Elias verily cometh first, and restoreth all things; and how it is written of the Son of man, that he must suffer many things, and be set at nought.

Hebrews 12:2 King James Version (KJV)

² Looking unto Jesus the author and finisher of our faith; who for the joy that was set before him endured the cross, despising the shame, and is set down at the right hand of the throne of God.

Mark 15:19 King James Version (KJV)

¹⁹ And they smote him on the head with a reed, and did spit upon him, and bowing their knees worshipped him.

Luke 8:53 King James Version (KJV)

⁵³ And they laughed him to scorn, knowing that she was dead.

Luke 9:22 King James Version (KJV)

²² Saying, The Son of man must suffer many things, and be rejected of the elders and chief priests and scribes, and be slain, and be raised the third day.

Luke 16:14 King James Version (KJV)

¹⁴ And the Pharisees also, who were covetous, heard all these things: and they derided him.

Psalm 69:29 King James Version (KJV)

²⁹ But I am poor and sorrowful: let thy salvation, O God, set me up on high.

Matthew 26:37 King James Version (KJV)

³⁷ And he took with him Peter and the two sons of Zebedee, and began to be sorrowful and very heavy.

Mark 14:34 King James Version (KJV)

³⁴ And saith unto them, My soul is exceeding sorrowful unto death: tarry ye here, and watch.

Hebrews 2:15 King James Version (KJV)

¹⁵ And deliver them who through fear of death were all their lifetime subject to bondage.

Hebrews 4:15 King James Version (KJV)

15 For we have not an high priest which cannot be touched with the feeling of our infirmities; but was in all points tempted like as we are, yet without sin.

Hebrews 5:7 King James Version (KJV)

7 Who in the days of his flesh, when he had offered up prayers and supplications with strong crying and tears unto him that was able to save him from death, and was heard in that he feared;

Zechariah 11:13 King James Version (KJV)

13 And the Lord said unto me, Cast it unto the potter: a goodly price that I was prised at of them. And I took the thirty pieces of silver, and cast them to the potter in the house of the Lord.

Matthew 27:9-10 King James Version (KJV)

9 Then was fulfilled that which was spoken by Jeremy the prophet, saying, And they took the thirty pieces of silver, the price of him that was valued, whom they of the children of Israel did value;

10 And gave them for the potter's field, as the Lord appointed me.

Acts 3:13-15 King James Version (KJV)

13 The God of Abraham, and of Isaac, and of Jacob, the God of our fathers, hath glorified his Son Jesus; whom ye delivered up, and denied him in the presence of Pilate, when he was determined to let him go.

14 But ye denied the Holy One and the Just, and desired a murderer to be granted unto you;

15 And killed the Prince of life, whom God hath raised from the dead; whereof we are witnesses. is despised and rejected of men; a man of sorrows, and acquainted with grief: and we hid as it were our faces from him; he was despised, and we esteemed him not.

WHAT CHRIST HAS DONE IS SO AMAZING!

He endured everything, the punishment that we earned as sinners; he suffered on the cross. His holy blood was spilled, and he died. Jesus completely paid our debt.

Evil spirits also know what Jesus did. They know that they do not have any legal rights and should leave; that they are broken.

Colossians 2:14

14 Blotting out the handwriting of ordinances that was against us, which was contrary to us, and took it out of the way, nailing it to his cross;

BUT... SOME DEMONS REMAIN HIDDEN!

Here is the truth! Those demons that stay and don't leave should be cast out. That is our work. That is why we have written this book of Deliverance, giving you the tools to do it.

We are tripartite, spirit, soul, and body. Demons live in our body and soul. Because of this, we suffer illness and pain. This happens both to those who believe in Christ, Christians, and those who do not.

As Christians, as children of God, we must cast them out. This book is for you, so that you have the tools of this Ministry of Deliverance and Healing. Practice them with yourself, your family and your congregation for the Glory of our Lord Jesus Christ. May He receive all of the honor, the glory, and the power forever and ever AMEN!

THINGS TO REMEMBER

- *Because thou hast hearkened unto the voice of thy wife, and hast eaten of the tree, of which I commanded thee, saying, Thou shalt not eat of it: Cursed is the ground for thy sake; in sorrow shalt thou eat of it all the days of thy life;*

- *For all have sinned and fall short of the glory of God*

- *Christ redeemed us from the Curse of the law, being made a Curse for us*

- *He bore our sickness and suffered our pain; and we had him flogged*

- *Then did they spit in his face, and buffeted him; and others smote him with the palms of their hands,*

- *He has taken the sin of many. On him is the iniquity of us all.*

7.
CONFERENCE OF DELIVERANCE

This conference took place in 2014, in Minnesota, USA

It may seem a lie! However, there are pastors who are opposed to deliverance. Even though Jesus did it, the apostles did it, Jesus gave them the order. So why don't they do it? Moreover, they criticize those who do. FALSE! They are blasphemers.

Luke 4:18-19

18 The Spirit of the Lord is upon me, because he hath anointed me to preach the gospel to the poor; he hath sent me to heal the brokenhearted, to preach deliverance to the captives, and recovering of sight to the blind, to set at liberty them that are bruised, 19 To preach the acceptable year of the Lord.

This was the mission that Jesus had on this earth. The Son of God came to undo the work of evil.

When Jesus refers to the poor, he speaks both on a spiritual and financial level. Brothers, we are all spiritually ruined, and he came to give us the good news; the Gospel. How many people grieve in their hearts? Brothers, I was one of them. Jesus came for these people. Freedom for the captive. So there are captives; under Satan we were captives. This message is for all of us. Jesus said, "As the Father sent me, I also send you."

Matthew 28:18-20

[18] And Jesus came and spake unto them, saying, All power is given unto me in heaven and in earth. 19 Go ye therefore, and teach all nations, baptizing them in the name of the Father, and of the Son, and of the Holy Ghost:20 Teaching them to observe all things whatsoever I have commanded you: and, lo, I am with you always, even unto the end of the world. Amen.

We speak about baptism, in the name of the Father, of the Son, and the Holy Spirit. When there is confusion among us, there are problems. The King of kings has plainly told us: in the Name of the Father, of the Son and the Holy Spirit. Amen. I emphasize this because there are brothers who have not asked to be freed, and what I often find with them is that they do not believe in the Trinity. There have been six people from different parts of the world who have practiced deliverance but have not been freed. What's more, the demons do not manifest, and I believe this is why. Do you know why? It is because the demons know the Word of God, and they know those who have right doctrine and those who don't.

> ***...demons know the Word of God and they know those who have good doctrine and those that don't.***

Luke 9:1

Then he called his twelve disciples together, and gave them power and authority over all devils, and to cure diseases.

It was clear. Jesus was sent to us to preach the kingdom of God, to heal sicknesses and to cast out demons. Announce the Gospel. Jesus has sent it equipped.

Matthew 10:5-8

5 These twelve Jesus sent forth, and commanded them, saying, Go not into the way of the Gentiles, and into any city of the Samaritans enter ye not: 6 But go rather to the lost sheep of the house of Israel. 7 And as ye go, preach, saying, The kingdom of heaven is at hand. 8 Heal the sick, cleanse the lepers, raise the dead, cast out devils: freely ye have received, freely give.

Jesus was very clear. If you are in need of deliverance, and you ask your pastor for help, he will not free you because he doesn't believe in deliverance, ask him why he doesn't believe if it is in the Bible. If he still refuses, go out and look for other brothers, because your church is mistaken. You decide what to do, to stay or to search for help from others. I would dare to say that this pastor has demons, and this is very common.

Mark 6:7, 12, 13,

7 And he called unto him the twelve, and began to send them forth by two and two; and gave them power over unclean spirits; 12 And they went out, and preached that men should repent. 13 And they cast out many devils, and anointed with oil many that were sick, and healed them.

Luke 9:37-42

37 And it came to pass, that on the next day, when they were come down from the hill, much people met him. 38 And, behold, a man of the company cried out, saying, Master, I beseech thee, look upon my son: for he is mine only child. 39 And, lo, a spirit taketh him, and he suddenly crieth out; and it teareth him that he foameth again, and bruising him hardly departeth from him. 40 And I besought thy disciples to cast him out; and they could not. 41 And Jesus answering said, O faithless and perverse generation, how long shall I be with you, and suffer you? Bring thy son hither. 42 And as he was yet a coming, the devil threw him down, and tare him. And Jesus rebuked the unclean spirit, and healed the child, and delivered him again to his father.

There are people who say there is no need to ask questions to a person or to demons. There are things we can not do, but that the Holy Spirit does for us. Amen. But Jesus did it before, and we follow him.

Once, Jesus asked, "How long has this girl been like this?" and the father responded, "Ever since she was a child."

Jesus healed the girl. In that case, Jesus explained to his disciples how to cast out demons. In fact, they were learning from Jesus. They also teach this to us, that is, how to learn. Prayer, fasting, and faith are essential, because of these, he call them an unbelieving generation. You must believe to be delivered, and you must also be free, Amen. Without faith, it is impossible to please God.

In Acts 1, Jesus Christ has died and risen again, and he says to the disciples:

Acts 1:8

8 But ye shall receive power, after that the Holy Ghost is come upon you: and ye shall be witnesses unto me both in Jerusalem, and in all Judaea, and in Samaria, and unto the uttermost part of the earth.

> **The power is in us through the Holy Spirit.**

Jesus said you would receive power when He comes, He within us; He is with us now. Amen? Therefore, we have power to do this work. Moreover, if we have the power, but we do not use it, it is as if we did not have it. If you have money and you do not use it (this is an example, not a comparison) it is as if you do not have it. Use it! The power is in us through the Holy Spirit.

Acts 5:16

16 There also came a multitude out of the cities round about unto Jerusalem, bringing sick folks, and them which were vexed with unclean spirits: and they were healed every one.

Acts 8:6-8 King James Version (KJV)

6 And the people with one accord gave heed unto those things which Philip spake, hearing and seeing the miracles which he did.

7 For unclean spirits, crying with loud voice, came out of many that were possessed with them: and many taken with palsies, and that were lame, were healed.

8 And there was great joy in that city.

Phillip was like us; Christian, pastor, leader. The question is whether your church practices deliverance. If not, talk with your pastor so that he can repent if he does not do it, and show him this book because it is possible that the congregation is sick.

> *...show him this book, because it is possible that the congregation is sick*

Why was there great joy in the city? Because everyone was healed. Why did people come? Because there were signs and miracles? Many came because they had dirty spirits.

Luke 13:10-17 King James Version (KJV)

10 And he was teaching in one of the synagogues on the sabbath.

11 And, behold, there was a woman which had a spirit of infirmity eighteen years, and was bowed together, and could in no wise lift up herself.

12 And when Jesus saw her, he called her to him, and said unto her, Woman, thou art loosed from thine infirmity.

13 And he laid his hands on her: and immediately she was made straight, and glorified God.

14 And the ruler of the synagogue answered with indignation, because that Jesus had healed on the sabbath day, and said unto the people, There are six days in which men ought to work: in them therefore come and be healed, and not on the sabbath day.

15 The Lord then answered him, and said, Thou hypocrite, doth not each one of you on the sabbath loose his ox or his ass from the stall, and lead him away to watering?

16 And ought not this woman, being a daughter of Abraham, whom Satan hath bound, lo, these eighteen years, be loosed from this bond on the sabbath day?

17 And when he had said these things, all his adversaries were ashamed: and all the people rejoiced for all the glorious things that were done by him.

There is a lesson here: there was a woman who was 18 years old with a SPIRIT OF SICKNESS! I wonder how many years she had been listening to various pastors and leaders. Jesus healed her of the demon, and no one did anything, not even the pastors.

This happens in most churches. There are many people who are sick because of demons, but no one does anything. That is why this is a book on deliverance; so that you are all trained in this area, and you can help others as they also help you. I had one similar case, a dear woman in our church spent more than 30 years with a hunchback, but she was freed from several demons in her back that were sent by a witchcraft. Jesus Christ is the same yesterday, today and forever!

The faith of the Canaanite woman.

Matthew 15:21-28

21 Then Jesus went thence, and departed into the coasts of Tyre and Sidon. 22 And, behold, a woman of Canaan came out of the same coasts, and cried unto him,

> *That is why this is a book on deliverance; so that you are all trained in this area and you can help others as they also help you.*

saying, Have mercy on me, O Lord, thou son of David; my daughter is grievously vexed with a devil. [23] But he answered her not a word. And his disciples came and besought him, saying, Send her away; for she crieth after us. [24] But he answered and said, I am not sent but unto the lost sheep of the house of Israel. [25] Then came she and worshipped him, saying, Lord, help me. [26] But he answered and said, It is not meet to take the children's bread, and to cast it to dogs. [27] And she said, Truth, Lord: yet the dogs eat of the crumbs which fall from their masters' table. [28] Then Jesus answered and said unto her, O woman, great is thy faith: be it unto thee even as thou wilt. And her daughter was made whole from that very hour

This woman was a foreigner, but when she humbly fell before the Lord, everything changed. This is the key! Deliverance is for those that believe, those that have faith. Those who have demons and do not have faith forget how to be freed. It is for the children of God.

The possessed Gergesene

Mark 5.1-20

1 And they came over unto the other side of the sea, into the country of the Gadarenes. 2 And when he was come out of the ship, immediately there met him out of the tombs a man with an unclean spirit, 3 Who had his dwelling among the tombs; and no man could bind him, no, not with chains: 4 Because that he had been often bound with fetters and chains, and the chains had been plucked asunder by him, and the fetters

> **This is the key! Deliverance is for those that believe, those that have faith.**

broken in pieces: neither could any man tame him. 5 And always, night and day, he was in the mountains, and in the tombs, crying, and cutting himself with stones. 6 But when he saw Jesus afar off, he ran and worshipped him, 7 And cried with a loud voice, and said, What have I to do with thee, Jesus, thou Son of the most high God? I adjure thee by God, that thou torment me not. 8 For he said unto him, Come out of the man, thou unclean spirit. 9 And he asked him, What is thy name? And he answered, saying, My name is Legion: for we are many. 10 And he besought him much that he would not send them away out of the country. 11 Now there was there nigh unto the mountains a great herd of swine feeding. 12 And all the devils besought him, saying, Send us into the swine, that we may enter into them. 13 And forthwith Jesus gave them leave. And the unclean spirits went out, and entered into the swine: and the herd ran violently down a steep place into the sea, (they were about two thousand;) and were choked in the sea. 14 And they that fed the swine fled, and told it in the city, and in the country. And they went out to see what it was that was done. 15 And they come to Jesus, and see him that was possessed with the devil, and had the legion, sitting, and clothed, and in his right mind: and they were afraid. 16 And they that saw it told them how it befell to him that was possessed with the devil, and also concerning the swine. 17 And they began to pray him to depart out of their coasts. 18 And when he was come into the ship, he that had been possessed with the devil prayed him that he might be with him. 19 Howbeit Jesus suffered him not, but saith unto him, Go home to thy friends, and tell them how great things the Lord hath done for thee, and hath had compassion on thee. 20 And he departed, and began to publish in Decapolis how great things Jesus had done for him: and all men did marvel.

This final passage is what we should do, in our churches and cities, the great things that Jesus does today. The devil lives in the grave; the demons are forced to live there.

The demons were living within the human being. No one could dominate them, but the Spirit of God that is within us. The demons recognize Jesus as the Son of High God. They run; they kneel; they know his authority, and they obey him. They know who we are and that we have authority in Jesus Christ.

> *Return home and tell of the great things that God has done.*

The demons do not want to go to the abyss. They search for bodies to occupy. They are tormented when they are cast out, so they search for bodies to live in. When they enter, they are free from torment, and they are in peace. However, when they are cast out. They are again tormented, and they leave the person in peace. The demons have names, and many of them are identified by what they do. There is always a leader.

> *The demons have names and many of them are identified by what they do.*

You are here to learn deliverance so that you can help others. So that you can help yourself. These things should be applied to you and your church. A leader always leads them, so you should ask for the demon that is above the others. This is crucial because, in some deliverance, a few demons leave and the people say that you are free, but that is not yet true. Some brothers and sisters are still left with a stronger one over them and they are shut up and hidden, and in this case, it could be the leader of a thousand demons or a legion of demons.

There are many who think, negotiate, make decisions, and respect authority. This is why the Name of Jesus is used to

> *80-90% of illness comes from demons.*

order this and that. When a Christian is on the side of Jesus, they listen. The demons are intelligent, and the demon that is inside us may have come from our past. They can also live in animals. Sin opens the door. Remove yourself from sin: Pornography, horror movies. 80-90% of illness comes from demons.

7.1. What is Deliverance?

It is the destruction of demons that reside within us. It is the work of freeing yourself from demons.

Why are there demons within us? They are here because there were or are open doors. There was a legal right for them to enter. Sin is one of those. They come to steal, kill, and destroy. This is why we must hate sin. It is important. Avoid sinning by watching unclean movies. They open these doors. They give a legal right to them to enter your body and soul. The problem is not the demon; it is the sin.

Deliverance is the labor or service within you through confession and repentance. It orders the demons to leave in the name of Jesus. Deliverance is to graze with our creator. With him and with his son. It will fix your life.

Moreover, the demons have to go in the Name of Jesus. Do we agree? They will not leave if we do not fix our lives if we are giving them a legal right to stay. Understand? Confess your sins from childhood and go to those you have hurt and ask for forgiveness. Give up what you should. These are simple examples. Do them.

I also have to forgive myself. This is deliverance. Everything is in the past; abortions, divorce, etc.

Many people do not go to church because of the hypocrisy that exists there. Brothers, I bless you, if you have never asked for forgiveness for what you have done, you should because you have caused harm.

I've told you that I had a business. I confidently believed until I went to a district attorney because someone would not pay me what he owed. One day, I ran into the person in Colombia, he had changed, and I told him I was a pastor. In my mind, I was telling him to pay me what he owed me, but I did not say anything. We have to fix our lives in order to be free.

I was also a womanizer and because of that I had many demons. I was freed, but the last demon that was a bit hidden was lust, it had not yet gone, but now it has, thanks to Jesus!

Adultery of the heart, do not look at other women with lust, this is adultery. Moreover, there are those who have been promiscuous. I renounced this and asked for forgiveness from God, and he freed me.

Pornography quickly takes us to masturbation. If we watch terrible things, demons enter through our eyes, and it is the same for what we listen to.

We can only cast out demons in the Name of Jesus. These signs follow those who believe: they can cast out demons and speak in tongues. The question is whether you believe in Christ. How many demons have been cast out? Pastor, do you believe in Christ? Yes, of course. Therefore, show me the signs of Christ. What signs? That the Name of Jesus can cast out demons.

> *We have to fix our lives in order to be free.*

When a person dies, the demons abandon its body. They can only live in a body that is alive, so they leave this body and search for another. Yes, they are searching for peace in your body, they will torment you. Do you understand, brothers? They will only leave in the Name of Jesus. Only through him and no other, as says the Word of God.

Demons understand authority, and they respect it. It is written and they know it. A characteristic of the believer is that they have these signs, and the signs of Jesus must follow you.

The Holy Spirit of God lives in our spirit. We are spirit, soul and body.

Demons try to live in a body because they do not have one; they are spirits.

As Christians, we are the property of God. We are the only ones who can be freed from demons.

We must leave our pride behind and become free. When pastors invited me to their churches, I asked if I can free them first, their wives, children, and leaders, and I asked if they'd stay by my side.

Jesus Christ wants His Word to reign in our lives abundantly, free from demons, free from sickness, free from storms, for his glory and honor, Jesus of Nazareth. Amen. Hallelujah.

THINGS TO REMEMBER

- *They will not go if you do not fix your life, if you are giving them a legal right to stay.*

- *We must leave behind our pride and become free.*

- *Demons know authority and they respect it, it is written and they know it.*

- *Only the name of Jesus can cast out demons.*

- *There are brothers who cannot be set free and what I have found is that they do not believe in the Trinity.*

- *Cast out demons; you have received, given by grace.*

- *The Son of God came to undo the work of evil.*

8. DELIVERANCE IN A CONFERENCE

The following information is related to a group of leaders in one of my seminaries in California who are part of a deliverance department. Use them as a model for individuals, groups, families or a church. Everything has been transcribed, word by word, from the video that was taken at this conference.

> *Note: The goal is to read this several times and adapt it.*

8.1. Introduction to total freedom.

Roger: First and foremost is to be at peace with the Lord, with others and with one's self.

After making a prayer of confession, renouncing and separating ourselves from sin, we must also get rid of our demos. We have just removed their legal right to influence us, since we know that the problem is sin.

You will be free in the name of Jesus Christ, but you must also maintain this freedom

You should not make the same mistakes that you made before. Be careful with what you watch on television or the Internet. Be careful with what you read in the news while you should be informed. Be cautious when reading about assassinations, rape, crime, terrorism, etc. The healthiest action we can take is to stay close to the Lord, to His Word, to his church, to the congregation, to teachings, and to the messages that Christ has given us and his Truth. Learn about what builds you up and less about what tears you down. Move closer to the Lord, as we move away from the things of this world that separate us from the calling and purpose of God. If you have friends, who do not believe in the Jesus Christ go and speak to them about the Lord. However, be careful that you do not get caught up in the problems of this person! Remember that the devil is constantly in pursuit and enters us through sin. Even when we are confident that nothing will happen. The devil is watching and following us wherever we are. In our anger, which is sin, he will enter. It is that simple.

> *"I always do it", every day of my life, I lift my prayer to lord asking forgiveness for whatever sin or word that I said and for the things I'm not aware of and for the casting out of any demons.*

Because of this, you must always stay alert and conscious of the war that we are in. "I always do it", every day of my life I lift my prayer to the Lord asking him forgiveness for whatever sin or word I've said and for the things I'm not aware of and for the casting out of any demons. If they want to enter through this area of my life, in the name of Jesus Christ I cast them out and they have to go. Every day I cancel whatever kind of Curse there is against me or my family in the name of Jesus Christ. We have the authority, and if we pay attention to the Work, we will have victory. If I am cleansed by the Lord Jesus Christ then no demon has power over my life; immediately I order them to withdraw from this place. It is simple. "Make it a routine."

"The demons," when they leave our body, usually they manifest themselves as burps, yawns, tears or vomiting.

They may speak through you. On some occasions, the devil will send information to your mind or vision, and you can tell me exactly when it happens. When you speak with someone, you know that there are many who are watching. Moreover, God is also watching and listening. Therefore, be careful with what you say and what you do. Another important thing! Never offend the demons. "NO!" The problem is sin. They are here because of sin. If anyone says an offensive thing to them, for example, "Damn demon!"... Ask for forgiveness to God for this. "NOT" to the demon. We are all creatures of God. If the devil came, he would not leave if you did not ask for forgiveness to God, and this is very serious. We will say a short prayer to destroy the curses that have possibly been made against us, our families or our ancestors. Stay calm, don't be afraid.

8.2. Massive Deliverance Prayer

Let's enter into the presence of Jesus Christ. Close your eyes so they do not distract you.

By the word of God, in the Name that is over all, the Name of Jesus Christ, I order the demons to fix all the damage they have caused to the believers of Jesus Christ. I order them in the Name of Jesus Christ. Whether health, work or whatever damage right now it is fixed. You caused the damage. You fix it.

These people have accepted, have recognized in their hearts that Jesus Christ is the Son of God, and they have confessed it with their mouths, that why all sins break. Your work is done! Leave these people immediately. You must; you do not have a choice, in the Name of Jesus Christ.

No demon can attack me. I am washed and covered in the Blood of Jesus Christ and full of the Holy Spirit and clothed in the armor of God. You have no authority over me. You are prohibited from attacking me in the Name of Jesus Christ.

These people have renounced all their sins, every demonic realm that is in these people, dissolve and leave them completely.

In the Name of Jesus Christ, also free these families, grandchildren, and parents. Remove every curse. In the Name of Jesus Christ, I take the sword that is the Word of God, and I speak blessings on this person and remove every curse that is over them.

In the name of Jesus Christ, I cut the chains, bonds, and ties.

In the name of Jesus Christ, this person is clean, and every curse is removed from it and its ancestors. Break every curse in the name of Jesus Christ. After this, all demons are left with nothing to do.

In the name of Jesus Christ who has already done all. I break all spells, satanic prayers, witchcraft with photos and of any type. Don't leave any relation, nothing similar.

> *No demon can attack me. I am washed and covered in the Blood of Jesus Christ and full of the Holy Spirit and clothed in the armor of God.*

If a demon has entered or has been sent through food or drink, break these orders in the Name of Jesus, bless that food, bless that drink in the Name of Jesus Christ, and all damage is cancelled, and the curse leaves.

If they have entered through a piece of clothing, an object, dirt, or anything else, I break this curse, in the Name of Jesus Christ I bless the garment, object or thing.

The demons leave because all the pacts are broken; the covenant that Jesus made annulled them. I bless their head, neck, back, stomach, private parts, and all the body.

Leave them! No demon stays! Totally leave, this person is free, they are Jesus'. All of them have to go.

There is not an option. It is the word of God. Out! It is an order in the Name of Jesus Christ. The sin has been confessed to the Lord. This person is forgiven. Not a single evil spirit is left because they no longer have any right to stay, in the name of Jesus they must go. If any demon has any legal right, I command them in the name of Jesus to show this person their legal right or motive for not wanting to leave. Moreover, in the name of Jesus, they are going to let these people ask forgiveness from God. Moreover, they are going to leave this person, Completely. You have no legal right. If you are here because of people that died, you must leave; you have to go. If you are here because of sickness, you have to get out of here. This person has renounced everything. If any demon thinks it has a legal right and doesn't want to leave, I command it to reveal to the person why it will not leave. In the name of Jesus, I command it. All demons that come from pride in this person confess mentally and ask for forgiveness from God and the demon that is listening has to go. OUT, OUT, OUT! IN THE NAME OF JESUS! OUT!

> *The demons leave because all the pacts are broken; the covenant that Jesus made annulled them.*
>
> *If any demon thinks it has a legal right and doesn't want to leave, I command it to reveal to the person why it won't leave.*

9.
GENERAL DOORWAYS OF DEMONIC ENTRANCES

Usually, there is common ways where demons come in; it is important to take into account these doors when you are doing the deliverance. Many are Biblical and others I have lived them myself or I have found them by my experience. I study in this area as well.

NOTE: For being an important topic, we will expand it in the next Chapter.

I clarify that we were redeemed by Jesus Christ from the curse of the law, the curse of the wickedness, of our sins and those from our ancestors, Gal 3:13. We are blessed, with grace, but the demons and the illnesses

But the demons and the illnesses do not simply go away; they stay with no legal rights in our bodies and those from our families, that's why we have diseases and suffering.

do not only go away; they stay with no legal rights in our bodies and those from our families, that's why we have diseases and suffering.

They make it real, that's why the key is to try, as possible, to know our sins and those from our ancestors, to be able to identify them, to renounce them and expel them quickly. Eradicate from our families: Curses of diabetes, cancer, alcoholism, poverty, and others; it is our duty to expel them all.

9.1. Generational Curses.

These are the curses that our fathers, grandfathers, great-grandfathers bring in our life, i.e. before we were born; you could have demons. These are called familiar demons; they are always inside your family. Examples: diseases, poverty, violence.

9.2. Own sins.

By disobeying God and his word: They are sins committed by ourselves.

9.3. Satanic agreements.

These are the agreements between a person and Satan or between people who want to achieve something for both benefits, so be it power, money, etc., they usually do it with animals' blood or human's blood, the person in return give Satan his family and his future generation spiritually.

9.4. Traumas, physical and emotional accidents.

The enemy takes any advantage to enter. The most common are through these traumas or accidents; they are the demons of sadness, bitterness, hatred, depression, fear and panic.

Examples: divorces, rapes, accidents, robberies, deaths, adulteries, infidelities.

9.5. By witchcraft.

This is a very common door, we have these cases in almost all of the deliverances, for this reason, we will dedicate a chapter to this subject below.

9.6. Curses by words:

We must be very careful with words we say or others say to us. I have found many people that have damaged their life because someone said to his or her parents that his or her children would be drug addicts and he or she really ending being that. Even the lyrics of the songs we heard or sing; there are lyrics of songs where people create bindings to us, especially the ones with sadness, spite and, of course, all that are not Christians. The most common words are: You will never get married! You will be nobody! You are an ignorant! You are a deadbeat! Etc.

9.7. Doors, special cases and testimonies.

These have been by my experience.

9.7.1. By attacking a Principality mistakenly.

It is not our duty to do it; we can ask a Father to do it in the Name of Jesus. He can do it, but we cannot. The problem is the sin, the agreement about a region that somebody has done, especially presidents, governors or any other person with authority could be the cause in that determined region. In that case, we must cancel the agreement in the name of Jesus and done! As simple as we solve the problem, we always have to remove the legal right and then expel it, it would be better if you know what was the agreement, but if you don't know, it doesn't matter; you can cancel everything by faith.

9.7.2. By breaking the supposed rights of the demons.

When a person has demons, usually, they take everything to your property and authority as theirs and they stand-up for it. In general, if a person has demons, they take everything under your possessions as theirs, or they think they have rights to several objects, and they defend it by attacking the intruder. Example: beds, clothes. Etc.

Testimony by breaking the supposed rights of the demons: I was once ministering a family in a room and I got tired, so I lied down on a bed that was there for several minutes, suddenly I had a strong attack from a demon that crossed to my right side to the left side of my chest to my heart and then it started to beat faster, it was tachycardia, and I reacted doing an auto-deliverance, but nothing happened, the demon won't let go, I started to get worried and running out of energy, the sister that was there started to pray but nothing happened, she was almost hysterical, the demon just won't go away. God sent me another of his servants with experience of deliverance and God used him to deliverance me; that was a big scare, although I know that they can't take my life without God's permission, and I was doing God's will. The problem was I let my guard down by no cleaning that bed spiritually; we must always do it when it is not our possession. Later, I found out that a young drug addict slept in that bed, and he had been taking drugs for three days like usual.

9.7.3. By nightmares (Sleeping).

Demons are ingenious and treacherous; they take any advantage to getting access to our bodies and torment us. I've discovered that they can enter our dreams and nightmares; they begin attacking our minds, all the time, especially in our dreams, when we can't defend ourselves for being sleeping, for this reason, it's very necessary always to pray and rebuke, this way we can achieve it even if we are dreaming or having nightmares. The Holy Spirit will remind us and even if we are sleeping, we can defend ourselves.

The most common are nightmares of fear, horror and panic or the ones with sexual content. Every time I have a nightmare or a dream, I rebuke, and if I wake up I keep rebuking. I have felt how they go out from my arm by moving unwittingly, and then I clean the room immediately.

In every ministration, I ask about this topic, and if they are repetitive, I ask them to tell me their dreams, and according to that, demons are expelled.

9.8. Typical doors of entrances to the demons.

These are some common ways we have found where demons get into our bodies; usually, a sin is the principal cause of entrance, actually, every sin we commit is a way in where demons can gain access.

Worship Saint Gregory
Abortions
Forced abortions
Accidents
Worship María Lionza
Catholicism
Gossip
Cigarette
Cocaine
Criticise
Holy devotions (Demons)
Drugs
Listen to Rock Music,
Listen to sermons about
Financial Property
Fornication
Fraud
Homosexuality
Horoscope
Idolatry people
Idolatry Saints
Imposition of hands no sanctified (in sin)
Wrath
Lust
Damnify
Marijuana
Horror, fair, war
Jehova's witnesses
Bring filthy objects to the house
Videogames
Raping Visit witches

Adultery
Martial Arts
Attack the Principalities
Bestialism
Witchcraft
Lie
Metallica
Fears
Mormon
No decimate
No forget
No respect demons
Novels
Occultism
Hatred
Batman's movies
Comedy and pornographic movies
Promise and not fulfill
Prostitution
Demonic agreements of blood
Fights
Ask for strength and power
Rebellion
Robbery
Satanism and hidden witchcraft
Yoga

MESSAGES TO REMEMBER

- *By witchcraft: This is a very common door, almost all of the deliverances, we have these cases.*
- *We must always take away the legal right and then expel them.*
- *For that reason, it's very necessary to always being praying and rebuking.*
- *I left my guard down by not cleaning that bed spiritually.*

10.
CONFERENCE ABOUT THE DOORWAYS

This conference was done in Minnesota, USA

We are going to talk about knowing the principal doors or doorways of demonic entrances in this part, when I say demonic, I almost always refer to diseases, where there are diseases, there are almost always demons, and where there are demons, there are diseases and destruction. About 80% or 90% is like that.

Then, there are four general ways where demons can enter, which you have to take into account when you are ministering the deliverances. I take those into account because they are the general doors where demons enter.

10.1. First Door: Generational Curses.

What are the Generational Curses? They are consequences of acts of our ancestors; fathers, grandfathers, and great-grandfathers. They have committed sins, and those sins have passed to us. Also, Generational Curses do not only come from the third or fourth generation, but from the tenth generation.

The Curse of the tenth generation directly deals with the Word of God about bastard children; they are those children who are born outside of marriage. We can say that many people have fallen there. A large part of humanity is related to this Curse; families, friends, neighbors. Currently, people commit sins of this nature than anything else. A man almost always has several women. They probably have a woman who is officially his wife, and also have many women hanging around, having children who are not born in a marriage. They are called bastard children. It is a sin committed at that moment and that Curse reaches the tenth generation, these are the Curses that demons do.

Right now, it is more common to see children born from a casual relationship, them from couples. They live together a while, then they break up when they think the relationship is over, or they just change partners. They live together without getting married, but they bring children to the world. Then, Curses are multiplied the evil increases.

Do you understand me? That is a typical example of a Generational curse up to ten generations. They passed one by one through generations of the people. Imagine that in each generation the same sin occurs. Which generation this curse would be cut out?

Among the Curses of Third and Fourth Generation, equally, we have that our ancestors committed sins of spiritual fornication, that is, they had other gods that weren't our Lord, despite the warning:

Exodus 20:1-6

"And God spoke all these words: I am the LORD your God, who brought you out of Egypt, out of the land of slavery. You shall have no other gods before me. You shall not make for yourself an image in the form of anything in heaven above or on the earth beneath or in

the waters below. You shall not bow down to them or worship them; for I, the LORD your God, am a jealous God, punishing the children for the sin of the parents to the third and fourth generation of those who hate me".

I ask: Do you see it clearly? Do you notice how it is to hate God? How and what is the idolatry?

The ancestors of people have many idolaters. Many people who worshiped images, sculptures, animals, people or objects, gods. God is jealous and strong, don't doubt about it.

Furthermore, we see that the iniquity of the parents upon the children is visited up to the Third and Fourth generation clearly.

10.2. Second Door: Our own sins.

The ones we committed consciously or unconsciously. This comes from our behavior.

Then, the only way to close this second door is through Christ. Who already deliveranced us at the Calvary's Cross. But now we have to cast out demons that entered by those sins.

10.3. Third Door: Traumas product of physical and emotional accidents.

Many demonic spirits of fear, horror and death come in as a result of car accidents, Also any other type of accidents. an abortion, an act of rape of a man or women. In either case demons enter. When we research someone's history, and we find out that their mother or grandmother were raped, it's likely that there are demons and those demons that entered their bodies still do some damage

> *They are the own sins, the ones we committed consciously or unconsciously.*

from one generation to another. Those are the physical and emotional traumas. Accidents and emotional traumas are very delicate. Accidents bring fears, sadness, tears, panic, horror, bitterness, wrath, anger and others. Those are evil spirits that entered the person and stayed to govern them. Do you realize? That is why the deliverance is important in the Name of the Lord Jesus; our King and Lord.

Although the emotional aspects are diverse in our entire life, we must have in mind that mistreating, beating, insulting, offending, deceiving a person, etc., bring as consequence demons as well, and through traumas they stay in the body of the people, siblings. We do not see the result of the traumas in the same day; usually, it takes a while to show what the demon has done in the person quietly. Do you understand? Therefore, remember; treat your friends well, your family, your neighbors, Even those who were your enemies. Then, how necessary is the deliverance in Christ?

10.4. Fourth Door: Curses sent by other people.

The mouth has power. Blessing and curses come depending on what we say. For example, other people send us Curses when they say to us: I hate you, you are a dummy. The dummy demon gets in there. You are lazy, you are good for nothing, you will not ever get married, you are nobody. All those words are curses that evil spirits do.

Let's talk here about witchcraft a bit, **Can witchcraft enter Christians?** No, it cannot. Any demon cannot enter inside them, when they believe in God. However, if the Christians commit a sin and someone else has sent them witchcraft, demons that were hanging around and waited the Christian to open the door can gain access.

Do you remember the demon that got out from that pastor? Witches joined forces, they did witchcraft on him, and they sent him demons. They tell us that they couldn't enter his body, but they make the Pastor research and search for what is the mind, the mind control and about subliminal messages through thoughts; and the way they could get access to his body. Thank God, he was deliveranced. Then, there are four giant doors. Demons gain access by those doors.

Well, I'm going to focus a little on **the generational doors**. It's a tremendous door that without thinking about it, a person is already born with demons, born with a tendency to act in certain ways or forms that oneself asks: Why do I act like this or why do I do this? For example: If you or your Dad are alcoholics or drug addicts, it is likely that there is a generational curse. Moreover, I assure you even if you are Christian, you have not been released from that demon, if you do not force it to get it out, it will pass to your children and grandchildren. All those things are a reality today.

I have many cases as I just have said, and it is true. From the majority of people who have been free, 95% of people were oppressed by demons for the sins of their ancestors.

If you don't get that demon that is there, it will pass to your children and grandchildren, all those things are a reality today.

10.4.1. A testimony from a mistress of 70 years old.

This is a woman of God, devoted to the things of God, who had had a very complicated life. She was living alone after having two marriage breakdowns and, furthermore. She had two daughters who lived separately from her, the thing was that none of this people wanted to know nothing about her. They rejected her. Then, when I try to release her from the demons, they talk to me, because demons can speak our language. One of them told me what happened to her family. Her dad had another woman before getting married to her mom, and He had children with her. This man did not get married to her, neither recognized his children and he left her. After that, this man got married and had children, what happened? That woman he had visited a witch (a woman who knows occultism), there are many witches anywhere. She did witchcraft on him, a curse of destruction on him and his descendant. The demon entered when she sent it there. Terrible! A whole life destroyed for this woman. Thank God, she was free, she was free. However, by then, she had destroyed most of her life. It is a whole life, 70 years.

The word of God says: If you obey my Word, you will be blessed, and everything you touch will be a great blessing, your land will be fertile. Everything is a blessing, there are not any diseases, everything is a blessing; but he also says: If you don't obey my Word, I will curse you, you shall not prosper, you will work and others will take the result of your labor, strange diseases will come after you, terminal diseases, and sores. He says all that. He also mentions the curse will reach the third and fourth generation.

Curses are a total reality, all the people suffer from curses; there are people constantly in anger. They appear to young people, but they are the result of the dad or mom who was grumpy, they are also demons that are there.

Remember that God made it all perfect. There are **homosexuals** who are boys. What happens is that the demon inside the homosexual makes him be attracted to the same sex or gender, to have a wrong sexual orientation. When the demon from that person is removed, he is released and becomes normal. I have had cases from men who were homosexuals, they subjected to a deliverance, and they were released, thank God; even one of them was going to get married. Then, what's the matter? There are homosexuals with demons that come from their ancestors. They come from their dad, mom or grandparents who were homosexuals. So the person is born with that problem, but by forcing the demon to get out, it ends right away.

There are acts where men have been raped at early ages, then the demon of rape gets into their body. The person becomes homosexual. The demon that is in there make the person to be homosexual, even many of them want to be normal again but they can't. Men of God who can't make it, many of them fight with their thoughts, emotions, memories and all those things, but the key is to get the demon out, with this done, thoughts and perturbation are over.

> *It's the responsibility of the pastors, the leaders of the church, to cast the demons out and heal the sick.*

The **Generational curses** are tremendous, brothers and sisters. If the person has not received deliverance, the demon could be in there. That is why we have to get the evil spirit out in the Name of Jesus.

The act of receiving Jesus Christi is tremendous! It's a great blessing, but it doesn't imply that the demon will go away. You have salvation and all that but the demon that is in there doesn't go away. It's the responsibility of the pastors, the leaders of the church to cast the demons out and heal the sick and that is delicate. Moreover, they are not doing it, and it is their responsibility. Yes, the generational curses are a palpable reality.

Consulting a witch is a sin and an open door for demons; the act is scary. If the demons have not been cast out, they keep being inside of the person. But thank God we have the authority in Christ to cast them out. That is the advantage of every releasing. What Jesus did at the Calvary's Cross is tremendous!

10.5. Common Doors.

10.5.1. About jokes and taunt.

These examples will give you clarity: If a person fell on the floor, and you laughed, brother, sister, you committed a sin there.

One question: Why do we not laugh if it is funny?; Because we do not have to do things of the old man. Be careful, don't laugh, help that person to stand up, we must be very careful. When one comes to Christ, it is utterly transformed.

For that reason, the sooner we know things about God, the sooner we avoid all these situations.

For that reason, the sooner we know things about God, the sooner we avoid all these situations. That man who fell off there, even if he doesn't know Jesus Christ. We should have a mind that Christ also paid a price for him. He loves him, Christ loves him, if that man doesn't know Jesus Christ, he is going to hell, worse, he will suffer more. Then, for that reason, brothers and sisters, don't laugh.

Example: You have a son, and he fell down. What do you do? Do you run immediately towards him to help him? Do you or do you not? Moreover, if someone laughs at your son who fell off, what would you do to that man who laughs at your son? Will you applaud and congratulate him because he laughed at your son? No! Now, we are sinners who defend our sons. The more our Lord, Who is Holy and Pure. It is necessary to be careful with those things, the simple act of mocking, opens doors, brothers, and sisters.

Let's see now, if a drunk falls on the floor and you laugh at him, the simple act of laughing is a great problem, brothers, and sisters. Don't laugh. If the drunk dies, the demon claims his right to follow you because you made fun of him. The things with God are very serious; He is Holy.

Now, the examples we have seen, I have discovered them with demons. I asked them, why are you here, demon? Moreover, they answered me: Because this woman laughed at the drunk. He died, and I follow her. Here I am, at that moment.

The things with God are very serious, remember. God with his mighty hand brought you out of Egypt, with signs and wonders, and yet. The people of God became rebellious and he said: You won't pass, none of you will get to the Promised Land, only the people in their twenties or younger are going to get there, the young ones. You all are going to die in the dessert if one is of God; we must have reverent fear before Him because He is Holy.

You say, Lord, forgive me in the name of Jesus. You keep doing the same. No, no. He is Holy.

Why are fights at homes? Money is not enough, business do not prosper, brothers and sisters, they are demons, by opening doors to them quietly.

10.5.2. The ignorance.

Do you know what is **breaking the territorial rights**? Where you tie, for example: I'm going to tie the principality of Minnesota, I'm going to tie them in the name of Jesus, I'm going to climb the hills, and we are going to make war against them. Brothers and sisters, you are doing something that you should not do, the divine law of God is establishing here. There are things you can do, and you should do, and others you cannot do and you should do. Things you can do and others you cannot do.

Satan. Who will destroy him? You will not. Jesus is who will do it; it is written in the book of the apocalypse, the Word of God. We have to deal with what is here, not from what is there. We know demons, principalities operate organized in this district or another, but, what's the matter? It is the sin.

Demons are consequences; they are results, the sin is the problem.

We have to leave the sin; Jesus died on the Calvary's Cross for that reason so that the sin could be removed through Jesus. What I did before; I was a womanizer; I do not do it anymore. I could not stop being a womanizer, I could not, that sin was in me, I could not, it had to be supernatural and Jesus took it away.

Here, I can be calm in this state, my wife can be calm, I was deliveranced, and I was free from the sin of being a womanizer. He is who takes away the sin of the world, Jesus Christ. Hallelujah! Thanks to Jesus! We have to love Him, brothers and sisters.

Then, territorial rights, no.

A sister I met in a town told me she was trying the principality of the town. When I asked her about it, she replied: We get up early to pray around 5 in the morning at the church. So I asked her. What do you pray for? She showed me a list, and when I saw it I said: Sister, this does not work like that.

Let's say a person does it, tie the principality, tied it forever, then there wouldn't be need to do it anymore, would it be? No, sister, this does not work like that; that is no tied. It would be too easy. Then, I explained this person that God does not send us to this kind of spiritual fights, which are improper. The fights we won are the ones that God send us to fight, we aren't responsible for those fights, we made a mistake going to fights which God hasn't sent us, we lose those fights, He protect us in his great mercy and all that, but we aren't responsible for those spiritual fights. Then, the sister told me with good reasons, now I understand why I had an accident on the motorbike and why my broomstick breaks every time. Of course, it was that she was doing something wrong. She did not commit a sin or something like that, but she was doing something that she was not responsible for.

We know the kingdom of darkness is organized, how is written in the book of Ephesians 6. For example, we cannot go in higher places if we did not conquer the smallest place yet. The Lord God delivered me from many curses of my ancestors. Now, it's necessary to govern our house first, and when we passed that level, if God allows us and leads us to a higher level, He won't expose us by doing things we can't do. He will not give us a burden we cannot carry.

They tell me: You explain to us that there are areas where we cannot enter, for example, tying principalities, legal authorities, governors, when demons of lower levels have not been expelled.

I tell them: Well, we should not do anything to those demons; you cannot mess with them because it is not established in the Word of God. Angels take care of them there, but you can ask the Lord, to intercede for a City, tie the enemy and the principalities, the Lord will do it. Don't get your life complicated. You have to intercede for this neighborhood, Lord, help us. The Lord does it, we are his sons and daughters, He does it in his mercy, and he does it in his time. However, you cannot do it. We can do it here for us directly, it is our right to do it, and we must do it.

However, we cannot do it on the territorial because they enter, they attack your life, and they can affect you. They torment you from every way, with your neighbors, with your boss at your job, friendships, etc.

There must be spiritual coverage to pray for you. Before coming here, the Church prayed and sent me here. I do not travel without asking a prayer, I do not if I do it, I probably have a demon of pride there. Humility is the key in this. You, brothers and sisters, talk with the Pastor or the Church in order to pray and send you to do the mission. At my church, I said to my siblings that they have to pray for me because I'm going to travel, and they pray, and then I travel but with the blessing of my siblings.

Same for you, please, always pray for me, I need prayer.

Well, now we know about the four principal doors, demons almost always come from those ways. **It's good and very important to know them**, because when we are doing an auto-deliverance or deliverance, we should attack these four parts: Generational Sins, Own Sins, Witchcraft and Traumas (physical and emotional accidents).

Now, I'm not going to talk much about the **own sins** because they are almost identical to the sins of our ancestors. Well, there are some **demonic agreements, demonic blood's agreements.** Dedications are made. You cannot know about it, but your grandfather or father could have practice witchcraft, Satanism, and is possible that they made an agreement or dedicated to Satan.

You belong to Jesus Christ now, but the demon is in you. That one that sent you when they made an agreement with blood. The blood's agreements are made from animal or human's blood. Where humans are sacrificed, they draw the blood and then make agreements that are dedicated to you. It is very common.

Hear this **testimony about demonic agreements.** When I started the ministery, the first case I found in the campaign was the singer of the Church and leader of worship. I told him to stop playing and take a step forward, alongside the others, so I could minister him as well because I include all the ministers when I do massive deliverances. Being a Pastor doesn't mean that you are free of demons. Forget about it.

> *Attack these four parts: Generational Sins, Own Sins, Witchcraft and Traumas, physical and emotional accidents.*

Demons focus more because they are ahead; then he sat down, luckily he was obedient (There are some who aren't, I met a Pastor who sat down just a moment, he stood up, and he left), this one was obedient, the demon he had inside was an agreed demon, saying its agreement was done between 4 and 7 years old by the grandfather. Moreover, I asked the demon, did you fulfill it? Yes, I did, he answered me, I fulfilled it, he is mine, and everything he has is mine, and I'm not going away because he is mine. Moreover, I question myself, how do I break a blood's agreement? I was about to give up, then I said to him, demon, step aside, I'm going to talk with Pedro (changed name); I want to talk with Pedro. I asked information about Pedro to the people around me and no one knew something about him, neither the Pastor knew anything about him. Then, I kept telling the demon to step aside that I was going to talk with Pedro; the demon did not obey me; he did not let Pedro speak up; he appeared at times saying. "Help me, help me", but then again the demon had the control of his body. Moreover, I said to myself: Oh my God, the demon will not go; I will stop here to finish it tomorrow. However, Pedro did not appear! The demon was raising there.

Then, God revealed to me "The agreement of blood of Jesus." One sees it simply, but the agreement of blood of Jesus has a tremendous and powerful significance.

When one reads the writing where Jesus says: ***"Because is in my Blood of the new agreement, which for many is shed for the remissions of the sins"***, you read it calmly, but that is tremendous! Powerful!

It was a tug of war with the demon, I lasted an hour and a half, being one o'clock at midnight; the service was very long. I was worried, and the demon kept telling me: I'm not going anywhere, he is mine. Moreover, I reminded the demon the blood's agreement of Jesus, and the demon that was violent and very aggressive lowered the head right away and left. I didn't notice when the demon was gone. Pedro was free, Glory to God. Of course, this happened when I was just starting the ministry. The agreement of blood of Jesus is tremendous. Pedro then told me, now I understand why I acted like I acted, why I did things I did not want to do. So, there are agreements of blood that people have received. Listen to me; if you have a family member who was or is a Satanist, brothers and sisters, listen to me, it's likely that an agreement was done to you, because they dedicate their family to Satan.

10.5.3. Be anxious.

It is also a sin that people do not pay attention. Brothers and sisters, what the Word of God says, that is it, and period. Not only we must obey the Ten Commandments, but there are also things that God says no, and it is no. For example, The Lord says, "Don't be anxious..." If you do it, you are not obeying him; you are committing a sin, and doing that a demon can enter your body. It is simple, there are people who devote here and there, even Pastors for doing the work of God; they are too much devoted. No, no, no, take it easy, take it easy.

> *But the agreement of blood of Jesus has a tremendous and powerful significance.*

Because the Lord says: Don't be too much devoted, and if you do it, you are disobeying his Word. Moreover, I have found that demon in a Co-Pastor for being here and there.

10.5.4. Unequally Yoked.

Do you know what is to be unequally yoked? The Lord says: "Don't be an unequal yoke." Do you see it? It is dangerous, and that means an awful marriage, if you are a Christian and you get married to someone who is not Christian, you are violating and letting in demons. Same goes for walking, doing business. Unequally yoked is in everything because the Lord says: "You cannot go in the darkness with light." Do you understand? There is a difference, Satan or the Kingdom of darkness cannot join with the kingdom of Light. You cannot be friend with people from other religions, you being a Christian with an unbeliever. That person belongs spiritually to the kingdom of darkness, and you belong to the kingdom of light. The demons are there since you are making a mistake, a sin; demons move to you.

I have found demons, where the woman was not a lesbian, but she had a demon of lesbianism inside her. The woman told me that when she was a little girl, she was a friend of a homosexual. Brothers and sisters, the demons move to that girl, and because of that, she started to have thoughts of looking for a woman. Did I ask her, are you lesbian? No, I'm not, she told me, but I have those lesbian thoughts. Then, demons move from person to person.

Unequally yoked, nothing to do in business, in everything and even worse in marriages. They say, I will get married, and I will convert her. I will convert him into Christian. No.

I have many cases as one of a woman, 20 years ago she started to go to the Church, she was recently converted to Christ, and a man began to attend to the service of the Church as well, in less than six months he fell in love with that woman and he pulled her out the Church.

What happened there? Who planned all that? The demon that told me the story (in the posterior deliverance), the one that was in there. The demon was telling me all the process (there is the video) A man was sent to a woman the demon says, he is mine. That man sang at the Church like any other Christian, the demon put a false love into him (Says the demon). She said to him that she would convert him into Christian, and I said (said the demon) who is going to convert him? The demon said who is going to convert him? It took 20 years of Christianity. The woman had a disastrous life. She didn't go to the Church anymore. The man was addicted to drugs, smoking marijuana in front of her. He arrived drunk every day. They didn't have a very common life. They had children who slept in different rooms. The man in his bedroom, and the woman slept in the living room on the sofa. There, a daughter of God with a disastrous life, thank God is now going back to the Church. Brothers and sisters, we have to be very careful. When the Lord says no, it is no.

10.5.5. The sins we committed in the past.

Of course, now you are not doing it, but you committed it in the past. Do you understand? If you did it in the past, brother or sister, the demon found a door there, and right now he is listening to me, the demon is there.

10.5.6. Witchcraft.

When you visit a witch, don't think its that one with a tail, or a witches' hat, no, no, no. There is no need to disguise the matter these days. Today they regular, it is enough to ask for someone who can do these "works".

All this affects you, and remember not only you, but all your descendants, since they put demons around you by committing a sin. Look how they work; they put demons on you, on your wife, your children, family members and neighbors in order to torment their life. Even at work, they put demons on you to torment you and like the majority of people are from this world, then, it is worse. That is why your boss pouts in order to destroy you, which is how they work.

but you committed it in the past. Do you understand? And if you did it in the past, brother or sister, the demon found a door there

Then, when you go to those witches, Oh! Brother, sister, you committed a sin against the Lord. We must regret it before the Lord in order to have that witchcraft removed. Business and others do this by reading hands. My sister, presented here, got a demon inside her by reading hands. It was so much that it injured her hand, she had a surgery and she still has some problems. I asked her, sister, how is your hand? She answered me. It is fine. So many years in problems, even though the insurance paid about 7 thousand dollars for you it was uncomfortable as well, and it was a simple sin she committed. These are things that happen to you. You are becoming aware of why there was opposition when I got here? When did you get here? Have you noticed? It is the devil does not want you to know these things, because knowledge is important, because "you will know the truth, and it will make you free". Moreover, you are free at this moment.

I will give you an example of witchcraft: A Sister from the Church called me saying that she believes her 10 years old son was bewitched, because he did everything with the hands together, the light bulb or flashlight, he walked while jumping, she thought that he was tied, she asked me for help to deliver him. I asked her: What do you think happened? She told me she remembered her son fought another kid from the school, who was oriental (Vietnamese or I don't remember), but she felt that they did something to her son. Then she took her son to the Church, and the demon manifested at the Church, someone has tied him, someone did witchcraft on him. The demon was gone and the problem was over, the kid became normal again.

There are a lot of doors that are sins, which are been committed, example: **Pornography, fornication, robberies, lies, tricks, jealousy, traps, fights, negative thoughts, bad words,** all those are sins, they are doors.

Participant - Pastor.

R.M. - Yes, tell me.

> **Participant** – Yes, I have homosexual friends, and I want to preach them the Word, but as I know and meet them, the problem is that I get together with them, right?
>
> **R.M.** - Yes, you must go and preach the Word, you must do it, but you being friends with them everywhere, no, nothing, because that is the problem. To preach them is right, we have to talk them about Christ, but neither can you cast out demons from an unbeliever.

It is important to know you cannot cast out demons from an unbeliever. Do you understand? Now you know a little of deliverance. Don't do it saying: Demon, leave this creature of God. No, don't do it. First, the person has to be of Christ. If you do it, it can cause you a problem, the demon follows you, wait the opportunity and attack you.

> **Participant**. - So, first comes the genuine acceptance of Christ.
>
> **R.M.** - Be Christian, go to Church and congregate. After that, they can be free, if not, you would have problems.
>
> **Participant**. - Then, if the person does not recognize Jesus Christ as his savior.
>
> **R.M.** - No. Within their heart, yes.
>
> **Participant**. What I have to do is to pray God for him.
>
> **R.M.** - Pray for him. Lord, have mercy on this person so he can know you. Thanks for the question.

During pregnancy, demons can enter as well. Be careful in the case where the couples fight at home, the child who is in there is a human being, he is alive, they perceive everything, they can hear, and the demons can also enter the child. Be very careful; Make him listen songs, praise, and things like that. Be very careful.

So during pregnancy many demons enter their bodies. There are times when the person got pregnant because mom and dad were drunk at the club for example, and she got pregnant. That is an unwanted pregnancy; then come demons of rejection, guilt, heartbreak, Etc. So that is delicate, do you realize? It is delicate. Was it love? Alternatively, was it an act of lust? Alternatively, it was simply that they liked making love, something like that.

You have to be very careful with that because spiritual beings enter the body of the child, such as heartbreaking and others like I said before. That is why there are children with low self-esteem, rebels and more. Then it is because spiritual beings entered their bodies since the beginning by fights, disagreements, etc.

It's important to know, you can't cast out demons from an unbeliever.

There are women who don't want to get pregnant and they get pregnant, so the husband realized that and left her, then she blames the baby, she make the baby guilty for the husband who left, causing rejection in the creature.

For that reason, when a woman is pregnant, she must take care of the babies and give them love, play praise music and all the good things that they can hear. If nobody cares about them, it can damage all their existence.

Many of us were conceived from different ways; we should ask our mothers, how do you conceive me and how I was born? In my case, my dad was married to another woman, imagine how I was conceived, all the demons my father had, they moved into me as well, fornication, adultery. They are generational, they moved into me and I had to cast out all those demons in the name of our Lord Jesus.

For that reason, Jesus became a curse. It is written "Cursed is everyone who is hung on a tree" He took all the curses of the people, also the iniquities that are the greatest sins and all the sins and diseases, to the Cross for our sake, so we can be free.

When you accept Jesus Christ, you will be free from all that automatically, because he paid for you, because you belong to Jesus. It is like you had been at the Cross; and actually the Word says "With Christ I am crucified, and I don't live, Christ lives in me", then everything stay on the cross, do you understand? So, there is no need to break the curse because Jesus did it. The sins you committed, Jesus took them away. However, now the sins we commit, like it or not, we sin because we are in the world, we can make mistakes, in something you don't want to commit, we must confess it right immediately, Lord I confess you the sin of anger and I ask for forgiveness, I was wrong; The Lord forgives you, and those curses are nullified right away, but the demon doesn't go away, do you understand? That demon from the curse does not go; we have to cast the demon out.

Let's see an example of the Pastor who is here, she is a Pastor, she was forgiven and all that, but she still have a generational demon inside her if no one hasn't forced the demon to leave.

Another example: On the videos I showed to you, the lady from Canada, a daughter of God, has the demon inside her. The curses were removed; everything was removed, but they stay in there. Now it is our job to cast them out.

Therefore, it's important to belong to Jesus Christ, because if the person is not, the curses keep going easily, and the demons stay in your body, and you can't cast them out because you don't belong to Jesus Christ. If you belong to him, you will qualify to be free because Jesus removed the curses. That is the good news; that is why you have to embrace Jesus, embrace Jesus Christ, brothers and sisters. Hallelujah!

However, remember, that is by faith, you have to believe, live and act according to that. When you have faith, you act, you move. I have faith, I act, I move, I save.

If I have a demon, I command him; you are going away in the name of Jesus. You are not going to say: demon, the Lord removed the sin, removed the curse, and nothing else, no. You have to take action: Demon, you are going away in the name of Jesus, and you are leaving because Jesus paid a price for me, he suffered, so I do not suffer. They know, and they will say: Ah! This believer has faith; I'm leaving, they said, and they leave immediately. Hallelujah, hallelujah, hallelujah!

In this ministry, I do not find that problem of wanting to know. What sin did my father or my ancestors commit in order to have this demon go away? Oh my God, how am I going to do to know it? Well, at least that demon said that the father did that, but what if there are other sins? How do I know? There is no need to know it because Jesus did it. Hallelujah! Jesus did everything at the Calvary's Cross. Hallelujah! Sure, of course! If you know what sins he committed, is so much easier to do the deliverance, which is why it is necessary to complete the deliverance's form.

That is why there are people who say: I cannot have demons because Jesus paid on the Calvary's Cross. Yes, they are right, and it is true, but you have to act, you have to cast out the demon that is inside you. Because that is how Pastors say: No, you cannot have demons or curses because Jesus took it all at the Cross, and they were true, and now, what? CAST THE DEMON OUT YOU HAVE IN THERE! Come, I cast them out in the name of Jesus, demon, in the name of Jesus; go away, and the demon left immediately. But if they don't do it, or worse, prevent someone to do it or prevent that the daughter of God to be free of demons by another servant or member of the Body of Christ, since we are one body.

10.5.7. Soap Operas.

Does someone watch soap operas? Did you watch soap operas in the past? Do you remember what novel was? Moreover, what was the name of the principal actor?

> *You are going to be free, you family's member, friends and others in their Churches.*

Well, it is likely that there is a demon with the same name there. Did someone watch Batman in the past? Did you see the principal actor in Batman? Is there someone named Chaky? He is a demon, we have found him. Brother, sister. Did someone watch the soap operas *The skin of the female toad*? The demon is named wild toad skin.

You don't watch soap operas now, but you did it in the past (Note, I'm not legalistic). Because it was a sin, you were committing a sin and you committed a sin then demons entered your body. Well, you

> *Don't be furious, be calm, oh right? Instead, start to pray; Lord, I forgave them.*

have to force the demon to leave, a soap operas brings many things, it has pornography, infidelities, fights, gossips, if not is it not a novel, because that is what people like. Almost all of us watched soap operas. For that reason, if you watched it you have to cast the demons out. The advantage: We belong to Jesus Christ, and we can be free. Hallelujah!

So you are learning things to be free; so you are going to be free, your family's members, friends and others in their Churches. Of course, it is going to be difficult because they will not believe you, and they will say that you are crazy. In your Church, discipline! Because you are a rebel for being in another place to pray. Tremendous brothers and sisters.

Like when Jesus drew demons in the Synagogues, what the religion leaders said. Don't come here on Saturdays to be healed, because it is forbidden! Do that another day. Hey, be glad because there is a servant who was 18 years hunched, and she was free. Hey, be glad! No, furious. Tremendous. Don't wait to give them a prize, no.

When I started this ministry, I knew I would find the opposition. When I told a fellow Christian that a person was sick for years in the bed and couldn't stand up, and I prayed in the name of Jesus, and the person stood up and walked right away. This person said indifferently: oh, yes. I said: Hey, won't you be glad! Hey, envy, jealousy rises! Brothers and sisters.

We have an example which is Jesus Christ; they did the same to Jesus. Brothers, sisters, they even killed him for that, for envy. Even Pilate knew about that; that was for envy. So, don't be furious, be calm, oh right? Instead, start to pray; Lord I forgave them, I forgave them because it is uncomfortable. Oh right?

You go to your Churches and say: I tell you that a brother from Seattle, Washington came, and he taught us things like that, and I am, happy and healthy, I was free, Pastor!

- Like that! Why did you go? With what permission did you go there? Ah, tremendous, my God, protect me, my God!

10.5.8. Horror movies, scary movies, war movies.

Oh my God! Who has seen war movies here? Oh my God. We all have seen war movies, Brother; here I have to give up to movies like Kaliman, the amazing man; Solín, patience; Mandrake; Which of you have seen Mandrake? A comic book, Mandrake, the magician. We have seen many movie. For example the movies like Batman, Superman, Etc.

10.5.9. Games at schools.

Example: I found the one with the pencil to be evil. They are two pencils. This game is played at the school,charlie pencil game, and the brother whom Jesus deliveranced did not play, but he saw it, and he also has the demon.

10.5.10. The Ouija board.

Very well-known! It is demonic. It is being asking questions to a demon from the future, present or past.

In Colombia, there was a **game with a glass and a ring** suspended, in where the questions were made saying, who will marry me? Won't I marry? The ring moved like a pendulum in different ways answering yes or not. They are all magic, doors that one made, or the parents made.

> **Participant**.- Brother, when I was 8 years old I lived with a lot of cousins and a rock girl arrived and lived with us in our house, she played the Ouija board a lot, but in paper, I didn't participate, but I was there looking.
>
> **R.M.** - There is a demon of the Ouija there. You, even if you did not participate, you were there. That is why is delicate, what we allow is a sin, that is why you have to get that away because is a sin. You allowed that by being there.
>
> **Participant**. - Is that a sin by another person?
>
> **R.M**. - No, it is not. That is an your own sin.
>
> **Participant**. - What about the people who played at the casino in the past?

All those things are demonic. All those things, gambling is demonic, demons of divination, we have to remove all those things, in the name of Jesus.

Then, the list is extensive

Do you have children? Who are married here? I will explain something to you here. **The parents are responsible for their house.** And if the woman is alone, she is responsible for her home because she is the spiritual authority. That also implies to have responsibility. Everything that happens in your house is your responsibility before God. If you have a son or someone grown-up at your home, and that person watches pornography, he is committing a sin, but you are committing a sin as well. You before God are equally responsible.

If your son have a computer to access the internet and he does wrong things, you are responsible, even if he is an adult, and he is living in your house; because he has to respect your house. Because your house must be holy because you are holy. No sin in your house, you are responsible, even though he is paying there. If not, your house is cursed, then it is delicate, it is a sin. You can pray, but you have to fix your home, all the things in the house and then you have to cast the demon out.

It happens a lot with your children, if they are rebels, you have to know everything that happens at your home. If you are the chief, you know everything that happens in your house and you have control over it, if you don't have the control in your house, there is a problem. There isn't leadership; and it's likely that they do wrong things at your home. This is frequently happening to the Christian people. The son or daughter is taking his or her friend, or girlfriend or boyfriend to their room and you allow it.

> *You are the authority. You must have control of everything that happens in your house.*

Brother, sister, have fear, He is Holy. He says: *"Be holy because I am holy."* We are chosen people, real priesthood. It is delicate, the matter is delicate. Then we must act so that the blessing come, sometimes we complain, why is it like that? We should seek the cause, the cause is the sin.

> **Participant**. - What can we do, brother? If one of our children or relatives have their own internet key. They have the right of having their things there, don't they?
>
> **R.M**. - You are the chief in your house. You are the authority. You must have control of everything that happens in your house. There is nothing you do not know. Moreover, if your younger son does something wrong there and the police find him, who is going to jail? Dad. Then, if it is like that in the secular, imagine it in the spiritual.
>
> **Participant.** - How old, brother?
>
> **R.M.** - It does not matter how old they are. You are in your house; you are responsible. Let's say that a man who is 50 years old is living in your house example, and he kills someone. What happen to you? First, you are interrogated; second, if it is possible that you knew something about his tendency to kill, you become an accomplice. Now, if it is like that in the secular, imagine it in the spiritual, if He is Holy. Keep your house in control and holiness, it has to be a home of God, has to be something holy, the temple of God, it has to be the Church of God, do you understand? The real church, it is accomplished. Take the control of everything, why? Because is our interest, because is the blessing of God.

Then, the kingdom of God is for those who take it by force. We must have authority, and to be the authority, and when we see they do not want to obey us, take the control. Moreover, if they resist or they object, you failed there. You have to talk to your son and say to him. Son, because I love you I take the control of this and the other, and if he resist, just take it away. You have to act; you have to act.

> *The kingdom of God is for those who take it by force. We must have authority, and to be the authoritarian.*

I love my son, but when we are in the car, sometimes he wants to talk about things that are against the Lord, I tell him: Son, in my car you are not going to talk about things against my Lord Jesus Christ. I forbid it. In my car you have to respect, I love my Lord, and you are not going to offend me, neither my wife nor the wife of Christ or my Christian music. Then, it's the same in my house, you won't see my son playing Nintendo, neither playing Pokémon, you won't see any of those things, neither if it is commanded by school, because in the school is commanded to read Harry Potter. Moreover, I forbade it. They called me at the school, and I went to talk with them.

They are not going to demonize my house. They are not going to do it for the sin, because God moves away, and the demons enter your house, in your life, in your marriage, in your family. Moreover, they are in there for a single sin, for not taking the things of God seriously, if God says no, it is no, at all costs.

Then, it is a delicate matter; you have to be very careful, but take care of your house, oh right? Be careful of being with quarrelsome people, we have to take care our testimony.

> **Participant.** - Brother, one question. We bought lottery before knowing God, Is it bad or it is not?

R.M. - Gambling. I also played many of them. We put our trust in God; He is the owner of the money and gold. We trust in Him.

R.M. - It is written in his Word, *"Consider how the wild flowers grow. They do not labor or spin. I tell you, not even Solomon in all his splendor was dressed like one of these"*. We depend on God, and if we put our trust in other things that aren't of God, we divert our faith.

Participant. - What happen in the separated homes when one of them teach the son the Word of God and the other does not?

Participant. - What can the believer do there?

R.M. - Pray. Well, brother, here we give family counseling for those cases, there are people who are like that product of the past because they didn't know the Word of God or they were unequally yoked, the Pastor says don't get married there and the other part ignores it and the result is that one of them want to baptize the Son in the Catholicism, full of images and idols, and the Christian doesn't want that. Or want to put the Virgin Maria here in my room or things like that. Just imagine it, all by the result of a wrong decision, but it has a solution.

10.5.11. Fighting video games.

There are many people demonized by video games. Parents, take control. There are parents who even buy all kind of video games to their children. In that field of video games we could preach all day. These doors are there. By giving a temporary happiness, you are demonizing your house. Most of these games are demonic.

10.5.12. Abortions.

There are abortions you committed, or you advised someone to do it. Today, abortions with pills of the Next Day are murdering innocent children. Every time you had sex and you were in your fertile period, it began the life of that creature, and the next day you took the pills, you killed the creature. That is murdering. I was also on that when I was in the world. God already forgave me for that, you know? This ministry is great, do you know why? Because you learn to fix your life, to confess your sins and to cast your demons out. You start a new life believing in Jesus Christ. Several people say: Hey, then there is a solution, yes, it is Jesus Christ. Hallelujah!

> **Participant**. - Brother, when one operates to not have babies.
>
> **R.M.** - Well, God is the one who gives life, God decides. That decision, it is a human choice, and that is the same to replace God. It is better to ask for forgiveness to the Lord. God makes the perfect work; it is better for husbands to work in their domain, the temperance, the rhythm method (when the woman is not in her fertile period).

10.5.13. The sexual act in wrong places of the body.

Each member of the body has its function. The purpose for which it was created, the anus is to defecate and nothing else! The mouth is for eating food! I have found demons that entered thru those places, and they were even getting sick. So if you have a sore throat, remember what you swallowed. Therefore, doing wrong things is a sin, be careful.

10.5.14. Raping are also doors.

By force or failed attempted. The game of the dad and mom are doors of sin. Then, there are inclinations o deviations since childhood. A sin is a sin.

10.5.15. Idolatry.

We have mentioned doors we see as NO Commons, plus another door that is the **idolatry of saints or people.** People who idolize people, singers, actors, the wife idolizes the husband or the husband the wife, or cars, or jobs.

It is taking the first place of God and giving it to the job, girlfriend, wife, children, hobbies, sports, Etc. If you continually leave the meetings at the Church for any other matter; there is idolatry.

Others doors are witchcraft, Satanism, Catholicism, horoscope, fornication, adultery, bestiality, sex with animals, lust, masturbation, pornography, homosexuality, prostitution, lesbianism. Many demons come thru this doors.

> *Each member of the body has its function, purpose for which it was created.*

10.5.16. Bringing filthy objects to home.

Although they are consciously or unconsciously brought to our home, they produce curses. Example: Dolls obtained from the vending machines. A person testifies that he received a doll, and it came possessed, because the owners of the machines made an agreement, then introducing it to the house carries a *curse*.

Although you pray and fast if this object is there, the demon does not go away, he is working with familiar fights, ruin, problems, Etc. What you have to do is to cast the demon out in the name of Jesus.

Well, everything that is **images** are curses, the Catholicism is full of these things, for example, the **rosary;** but the faithful do not know it. Also pictures of **oriental objects.** Most of the Hindu objects are things dedicated to their Gods. Demons are around the objects, not inside. They live in a place where the object is.

Elephants for luck, Buddha, Chests. These are elements that are dedicated to pagan gods.

Many indigenous things in Mexico; and also in others countries. The ax, the horseshoe, the aloe bush. They are all those things that I saw and lived when I was in the world.

You can be sure that there are demons around these things.

Testimony from a woman whose son was seven years old had epileptic attacks; he fell off the stairs at the school. She lived in France, I recommended her to take out a whole series of objects, she was Catholic; and the day she took out all the objects and images she had in her house, the child was healed. He never had more attacks.

This demons are not playing, and God does not play. When God says take that out, take that out!

When God told the Israel people to leave Egypt, that he was in the front; when you go there, destroy all those bad habits and don't give your sons and daughters, because then they will be learning the pagan customs, they will worship the idols and they will invite you to eat the food dedicated to these idols. That is anathema; it is a sin.

That is delicate, don't bring objects to your house, nothing, zero. Don't accept others stories,

> *The day she took out all the objects and images she had in her house, the child was healed.*

when you arrive at your home, clean it and don't have improper pictures or objects. I have a sermon of how to clean your house and the church.

> *To learn about wickedness you don't have to go to school or college.*

An example: one friend gave her a doll, but do you know that her friend had envy for her husband, and you keep the gift because is cute or to remember your friend. Be sure that the gift came with a curse. Don't believe that story. It is likely that her friend made a prayer to destroy her home, or finances, or something. Take out that gift, destroy it, don't give it to another person, do not pass the curse, and cast the demon out before it is too late. That is witchcraft; they are delicate things.

10.5.17. The clothes you wear – Take care of your house.

You have to know what it is written on your clothes; if you do not know because it is written in another language, it is better to ask about it or don't wear those clothes. Someone gave my wife a gift, and she asked for them. I said: I threw it away because I saw something strange in that doll; I'm responsible for the house. I take care of the house!

You have to clean all your houses, I suggest not having many things on the walls that you bought without knowing, many of them can be dedicated. You must be alert.

These are real things, to learn about the wickedness, you do not have to go to school or college, it's there, many times there is no need to pay, and this can be taught anywhere.

10.5.18. Curse Words – Cursing.

Which is not only saying: I curse you. No: Cursing is saying something bad to someone.

Examples:

- You are dumb
- You are good for nothing
- You are a jerk
- You are not going to get married
- You always do everything worse
- Your cooking is bad

- You are fat
- You are skinny
- You have bad luck
- You are a bastard
- You are miserable
- Damn you, Etc.

It seems simple and normal, but it is not, you are sentencing that person. You went to school and didn't pass the test, and the teacher said "You are stupid!" You get inside a demon of stupid. In fact, nobody likes to hear something bad about oneself, even when it is with affection.

Examples:

- My chubby
- My nigga

- My old man
- My chinchilla, Etc.

We must change the language, we bless, that everything we say is good, that people get blessed by our mouth

Examples:

- You are responsible
- You are smart
- How sweet you are, Etc.

> **God says:** *"Be holy because I am holy." Remember, "He moved us from the kingdom of darkness to the kingdom of light", "We are light, we are lamps", "Holy Nation, real priesthood", and we have to act like that. "With Christ I am together crucified, and I do not live anymore, Christ lives in me," "The old things happened, Here everything is new."*

"So we walk in this world" "not to do my will, but to do the will of who sent me", not my word, but the Word of him, not my language, but the language of Him, not the one from my neighbor, but the one that belongs to Him. What the Word of God says is what I am going to say.

> **Participant**.- Pastor, when someone lives with her parents, single, without knowing God, and get pregnant by the boyfriend, and decided to leave her home; the parents get mad, and they mistreat her, with angry, and they said to her angry words, sharp words, many words to the child, Is that curse?
>
> **R.M**. - Of course, they are cursing. One thing is getting mad, and another thing is letting go of anger
>
> **R.M**. - *"Get angry but don't commit a sin"*. However, if I keep saying bad words, I am still cursing. If I get mad, I ask for forgiveness to God, to the person, and I forgive myself, and I keep walking with Faith.
>
> **Participant**. - If the young girl that got pregnant was not there and didn't listen to the parent's anger words directly. Is that a curse too?
>
> **R.M**. - Of course, it is a curse. Because, first, she offended her parents with the pregnancy out of marriage. Second, she left her home without such consent. In both cases, she offended God and her parents. So, the demons will take charge of disturbing the baby and the new parents. Remember what the Lord said: You have who accused you, Moses (The law) *"Honor your father, and your mother, then your days will be longer*

> *What the Word of God says is what I am going to say.*

and full of prosperity, which is the first commandment with a promise".

Do you see? So, who do you think will execute the curse? Sure, the demons. Now, well, although you did not listen his curse words, this was sent and next to it the demons to execute it.

The spiritual world is very fragile; that is why you have to make the peace with all the people. E.g.: a person is in another country and he sent us curses, if we aren't with Christ, this will affect us, but if we are walking in the Holiness in Christ, we can't be affected. Then, if the person cursed, the demons went to execute it, if the person bless, wherever the person is, will be blessed by the angels.

Despite having the privilege to have Jesus, and He forgive us, we must stay clean, asking forgiveness for the things we do know that it is not all right. Moreover, forgiving who made a mistake with us.

> **We have to search for the cause, everything has a cause.**

There are people who say or sing I crush your head, Satan. These things do not have to be said. There are people that deal with the demons because the fight with his partner and there is no need for this, everything has its order. The demon says: What fault have I, if the person goes with pornographic, cursing and with sin.

I am here because I was sent. (Thus they say to me in the releases) Who sent you? John Doe. Why did he send you? Because this person made this and the other. They are accomplishing. We have to search the cause; everything has a cause.

We must be careful and be in holiness to cast these demons out.

10.5.19. Imposing hands, being in sin.

It is also delicate because the other person can be full of demons and is very likely that those demons move to you and yours to that person. You, brother, if you see that the leader, which is under authority, is in Sin don't let impose hand from him, There are sins that are easy to discover, such as, if you see that that leader or pastor is violent, proud, angry or is with look of lust or any hint, please don't let him put his hands in your head, because being in that position of submission under the leader of the authority, demons take advantage of that and some can get inside of you, and when you let your guard down, you do or practice that sin from the Leader.

> "Do not lay hands upon anyone too hastily and thereby share responsibility for the sins of others; keep yourself free from sin," 1 Tim. 5:22

Not everyone, they haven't been fully released and demons of lust, pride, divisions appear with them.

For example: One person said to the Pastor (before being a believer), that your business would be prospered, and you imposed hands, and the result was that his business collapsed, he sent a demon who was out today. I found Church's leaders placing demons, demonizing many people. All the people whom these leaders laid hands from were affected. I have been liberating many of them.

> **Participant**. - The Pastor is the one who has to lay hands, right?
>
> **R.M**. - Yes, but it could be others leaders. However, be careful, if you see a Pastor with anger, brother; don't let

him lay hands on you. Part of those demons move to you.

Example: If a Pastor is in adultery, it is likely that the others leaders and members have demons as well because they are under the authority of that Pastor and the demons have been transferred to them. That Church is full of demons.

There are also Pastors who are in fights and wanting to divorce; then the demon of divorce get inside of the Church and at the Church, there, the brothers and sisters start to divorce. Or, if gossiping begins, everyone at the Church gossip.

Be very careful with the people you bring to the Church, either evangelist or singers because many of them, not everyone, haven't been fully released, and demons of lust, pride, divisions appear to them.

You have to be careful, in the Church where I get together with other people, not everyone lay hands, not everyone can serve, the person must be holy and either his house, walking correctly.

It's very common to see a Church that bring evangelist or singers doing campaigns without studying their personal life, their fruits and if we later note there is discord or problems inside the Church, possibly the cause was the arrival of that person. They could have brought the demon. Furthermore, many don't think that a Christian could have demons. The pastor has full responsibility in the Church in the caring of the sheep of the Lord. Not everyone can lay hands, more like putting demons.

You have to be careful. The Church where I get together with others is growing because people see there is holiness, transformation and signs and wonders, the women who could not have children, now all of them have children. People heard good Word, and they are transformed with many signs and wonders. The Word works transforms and heals.

10.5.20. The no-Tithe

If you tithe, you are under blessing. As long as you are with incomes, you have to give what is not yours, you must tithe, and what is yours, keep it to yourself and manage it in a good way. And if there something you can give to God, that is an offering, then you are going to give him an offering, and if you want to support this ministry of Christ deliverances of Roger D Muñoz, support it. I have found several demons by not tithing.

10.5.21. Drug addiction.

The drugs such as the cocaine, the marijuana, cigarettes, etc.

10.5.22. Sermons of financial prosperity.

It is more than likely that those demons are going to enter your body, and they will make you love money; I have found many of them.

10.5.23. Promising and not fulfilling.

Example: if the Pastor asks for help for something at the Church, and you say I can do it, knowing you cannot, it is better to say no, and being right with God. Because my Lord is Holy.

10.5.24. General Music World

Rock, Michael Jackson's music, when I was in the world I listened to Michael Jackson, and I had to ask for forgiveness to the Lord and I commanded the demons to get out and they had to obey. Remember the lyrics of grief, sadness, rebellion, lust, lewdness, blasphemy, grudges, hatred, shame, revenge, and others that are in the song's lyrics

10.5.25. Other doors:

- Not forgive
- Robbery
- Wrath
- Criticizing
- Yoga
- Martial arts
- Gossip
- Sects, Jehovah's Witnesses
- Mormonism
- Ask for strength and power in the wrong place
- People who go to the gym or practice Zumba, be careful with the sexy moves.

MESSAGES TO REMEMBER

- *Where there are diseases, there are almost always demons, and where there are demons there are diseases.*
- *They are consequences from acts of our ancestors, the parents, grandparents, great-grandparents, they have committed sins, and those sins have passed to us.*
- *Traumas that are product of accidents or physical emotions are access for demons*
- *Depending on what we talk, Curses enter without thinking, or people tell us words and those words are curses.*
- *There are people that go with anger, you can see this a lot in young people, but this is the result of an angry father, angry mother. They also are demons that stand there*
- *The problem is the sin, we must quit the sin, and for that, Jesus died at the Calvary's Cross*
- *You say, Lord forgive me in the name of Jesus. And you keep doing the same. No, no. He is Holy*
- *He won't give us burdens that we cannot carry on*
- *If you have a family that was or is Satanist, brother, sister, listen to me well, there is a huge possibility that there is an agreement, because they devote their family to Satan*

11.
CREATION OF A DELIVERANCE TEAM

It is vital that each church establish a deliverance team to minister its members and the pastoral family. They are here to serve the whole Body of Christ. In this chapter, you'll find the steps to create this essential team.

11.1. Primary Characteristics of a Deliverance Ministry.

As all ministries and secular will work, it is necessary that you create an outline that allows someone to do their work without becoming emotionally compromised. Of course, once the work has started, it will continue to evolve through the guidance of the Holy Spirit to whom we must always be sensitive and act with a clear conscience, sincerity, social responsibility and Love.

The practice of the deliverance ministry is nothing new nor is it a novelty. It is a ministry that requires significant responsibility as you enter the spiritual realm and begin to see the reality of the human situation with respect to good and evil and in relation to the state of abundant life and the poverty in

> *It is a ministry that requires significant responsibility as you enter the spiritual realm*

which we actually live. We begin to see the roots that must be uprooted and face the sower who planted them.

The good news is that this simple sower, named Satan, can do nothing when the ruler of the world has ordered that it be cleaned through the Blood of Christ. This was sufficient for the work to be done.

The ruler of the universe, the giver of life and liberty, and most of all, the Blood cleaner, once recognized, demonstrates his power and begins to value us as much as precious gold. As children of God, we have value, not because of our little faith, but because we begin to appreciate the incredible liberty that we find in Christ.

Let us then begin to analyze which people should participate in this ministries by looking at the instructions in our life manual, the Bible.

In this chapter, as in this entire book, we will use the King James Version.

KJV Acts 19:13-20

13 Then certain of the vagabond Jews, exorcists, took upon them to call over them which had evil spirits the name of the Lord Jesus, saying, We adjure you by Jesus whom Paul preacheth. 14 And there were seven sons of one Sceva, a Jew, and chief of the priests, which did so. 15 And the evil spirit answered and said, Jesus I know, and Paul I know; but who are ye? 16 And the man in whom the evil spirit was leaped on them, and overcame them, and prevailed against them, so that they fled out of that house naked and wounded. 17 And this was known to all the Jews and Greeks also dwelling at Ephesus; and fear fell on them all, and the name of the Lord Jesus was magnified. 18 And many that believed came, and confessed, and shewed their deeds. 19 Many of them also which used curious arts brought their books together, and burned them before all men: and they counted the price of them, and found it fifty thousand pieces of silver. 20 So mightily grew the word of God and prevailed.

Not all people should serve in the ministry of deliverance because of the seriousness of the situations they will be involved with. Those who wish to be dedicated to this ministry should understand the delicacy of the situation and the responsibility and sanctity that is required.

We must understand that the Blood of Jesus not only returns us to life, but also makes us children of God and returns our liberty by freeing us from the captivity of sin.

KJV Romans 6:8-14

Now if we be dead with Christ, we believe that we shall also live with him: 9 Knowing that Christ being raised from the dead dieth no more; death hath no more dominion over him. 10 For in that he died, he died unto sin once: but in that he liveth, he liveth unto God. 11 Likewise reckon ye also yourselves to be dead indeed unto sin, but alive unto God through Jesus Christ our Lord. 12 Let not sin therefore reign in your mortal body, that ye should obey it in the lusts thereof. 13 Neither yield ye your members as instruments of unrighteousness unto sin: but yield yourselves unto God, as those that are alive from the dead, and your members as instruments of righteousness unto God. 14 For sin shall not have dominion over you: for ye are not under the law, but under grace.

The particular view that we use to cast out demons or dedicate ourselves to this branch requires us to choose special people so that they will not be praised more than they should. Humility is very necessary as we continue and hold only to the power of Jesus Christ and his Blood, shed for us. It is his power that allows us to do these practices of giving freedom to the oppressed, bound, and subjugated.

If it is true that our freedom comes from Christ, then we know that evil only comes to kill, rob, and destroy, and it continues to influence Christian illegally. Because of this, we must clean our bodies and souls although not our spirits since this has already been done. This is called the new birth and in an instant; the Holy Spirit enters us to dwell united with our reborn spirit.

Only Christians should serve in this ministry. It is important to remember that those who do not belong to Christ, who are children of this world, should not serve in this ministry. The kingdom cannot be divided, and this person is not free because they remain a slave to sin. Their spirit continues to die because it is governed by this world.

We have been called to give freedom to those who already have the right and authority to belong to God. Evil no longer has a place in the children of God, and, therefore, our ministry can continue with full freedom and authority.

In Luke, Jesus describes this ministry, the purpose for which he came to this world.

> *We have been called to give freedom to those who already have the right and authority to belong to God. Evil no longer has a place in the children of God*

KJV Luke 4:17 – 21

[17] *And there was delivered unto him the book of the prophet Esaias. And when he had opened the book, he*

found the place where it was written, 18 The Spirit of the Lord is upon me, because he hath anointed me to preach the gospel to the poor; he hath sent me to heal the brokenhearted, to preach deliverance to the captives, and recovering of sight to the blind, to set at liberty them that are bruised, 19 To preach the acceptable year of the Lord. 20 And he closed the book, and he gave it again to the minister, and sat down. And the eyes of all them that were in the synagogue were fastened on him. 21 And he began to say unto them, This day is this scripture fulfilled in your ears.

11.2. Be Born Again.

KJV John 3 1-8

There was a man of the Pharisees, named Nicodemus, a ruler of the Jews: 2 The same came to Jesus by night, and said unto him, Rabbi, we know that thou art a teacher come from God: for no man can do these miracles that thou doest, except God be with him. 3 Jesus answered and said unto him, Verily, verily, I say unto thee, Except a man be born again, he cannot see the kingdom of God. 4 Nicodemus saith unto him, How can a man be born when he is old? can he enter the second time into his mother's womb, and be born? 5 Jesus answered, Verily, verily, I say unto thee, Except a man be born of water and of the Spirit, he cannot enter into the kingdom of God. 6 That which is born of the flesh is flesh; and that which is born of the Spirit is spirit. 7 Marvel not that I said unto thee, Ye must be born again. 8 The wind bloweth where it listeth, and thou hearest the sound thereof, but canst not tell whence it cometh, and whither it goeth: so is every one that is born of the Spirit.

The New birth is required in order to acknowledge Jesus Christ as the only Savior and to recognize that his Blood, shed on the Cross, was a sufficient sacrifice to return us to life in the spirit. Because of the disobedience of man (Adam), we were dead, and because of the multitude of sins of man, we needed this sacrifice in order to receive freedom. God sent his son, who through his suffering, became obedient, and through this suffering and obedience, we were saved and He was exalted.

KJV Acts 2:38

38 Then Peter said unto them, Repent, and be baptized every one of you in the name of Jesus Christ for the remission of sins, and ye shall receive the gift of the Holy Ghost.

The work of the Lord is done completely through his grace.

KJV...Ephesians 2:1-10

And you hath he quickened, who were dead in trespasses and sins; 2 Wherein in time past ye walked according to the course of this world, according to the prince of the power of the air, the spirit that now worketh in the children of disobedience: 3 Among whom also we all had our conversation in times past in the lusts of our flesh, fulfilling the desires of the flesh and of the mind; and were by nature the children of wrath, even as others. 4 But God, who is rich in mercy, for his great love wherewith he loved us, 5 Even when we were dead in sins, hath quickened us together with Christ, (by grace ye are saved;) 6 And hath raised us up together, and made us sit together in heavenly places in Christ Jesus: 7 That in the ages to come he might shew the exceeding riches of his grace in his kindness toward us through Christ

Jesus. 8 For by grace are ye saved through faith; and that not of yourselves: it is the gift of God: 9 Not of works, lest any man should boast. 10 For we are his workmanship, created in Christ Jesus unto good works, which God hath before ordained that we should walk in them.

New birth makes us new creatures and removes all of our past.

KJV 2 Corinthians 5 17-21

17 Therefore if any man be in Christ, he is a new creature: old things are passed away; behold, all things are become new. 18 And all things are of God, who hath reconciled us to himself by Jesus Christ, and hath given to us the ministry of reconciliation; 19 To wit, that God was in Christ, reconciling the world unto himself, not imputing their trespasses unto them; and hath committed unto us the word of reconciliation. 20 Now then we are ambassadors for Christ, as though God did beseech you by us: we pray you in Christ's stead, be ye reconciled to God. 21 For he hath made him to be sin for us, who knew no sin; that we might be made the righteousness of God in him.

Knowing that our spirit lives and is united with the Holy Spirit that guides us, putting our faith in the future hope of our salvation

KJV 1 Peter 1:3-5

Blessed be the God and Father of our Lord Jesus Christ, which according to his abundant mercy hath begotten us again unto a lively hope by the resurrection of Jesus Christ from the dead, 4 To an inheritance incorruptible, and undefiled, and that fadeth not away, reserved in heaven for you, 5 Who are kept by the power of God through faith unto salvation ready to be revealed in the last time.

We are temples of the Holy Spirit.

KJV 1 Corinthians 6:19- 20.

19 What? know ye not that your body is the temple of the Holy Ghost which is in you, which ye have of God, and ye are not your own? 20 For ye are bought with a price: therefore glorify God in your body, and in your spirit, which are God's.

The Holy Spirit guides us into all truth

John 16:7-15 King James Version (KJV)

7 Nevertheless I tell you the truth; It is expedient for you that I go away: for if I go not away, the Comforter will not come unto you; but if I depart, I will send him unto you.

8 And when he is come, he will reprove the world of sin, and of righteousness, and of judgment:

9 Of sin, because they believe not on me;

10 Of righteousness, because I go to my Father, and ye see me no more;

11 Of judgment, because the prince of this world is judged.

12 I have yet many things to say unto you, but ye cannot bear them now.

¹³ Howbeit when he, the Spirit of truth, is come, he will guide you into all truth: for he shall not speak of himself; but whatsoever he shall hear, that shall he speak: and he will shew you things to come.

¹⁴ He shall glorify me: for he shall receive of mine, and shall shew it unto you.

¹⁵ All things that the Father hath are mine: therefore said I, that he shall take of mine, and shall shew it unto you.

The Holy Spirit is the evidence in our lives of our future redemption

Ephesians 1:13-14

¹³ In whom ye also trusted, after that ye heard the word of truth, the gospel of your salvation: in whom also after that ye believed, ye were sealed with that holy Spirit of promise,14 Which is the earnest of our inheritance until the redemption of the purchased possession, unto the praise of his glory.

11.3 Be a Genuine Disciple of Christ.

We must obey his will first and fulfill our social and financial obligations to the church, loving our neighbor, and perfecting one another in love.

KJV John 15: 7 -17

⁷ If ye abide in me, and my words abide in you, ye shall ask what ye will, and it shall be done unto you. 8 Herein is my Father glorified, that ye bear much fruit; so shall ye be my disciples. 9 As the Father hath loved me, so have I loved you: continue ye in my love. 10 If ye keep my commandments, ye shall abide in my love; even as I have kept my Father's commandments, and abide in his love. 11 These things have I spoken unto you, that my joy might remain in you, and that your joy might be full. 12 This is my commandment, That ye love one another, as I have loved you. 13 Greater love hath no man than this, that a man lay down his life for his friends. 14 Ye are my friends, if ye do whatsoever I command you. 15 Henceforth I call you not servants; for the servant knoweth not what his lord doeth: but I have called you friends; for all things that I have heard of my Father I have made known unto you. 16 Ye have not chosen me, but I have chosen you, and ordained you, that ye should go and bring forth fruit, and that your fruit should remain: that whatsoever ye shall ask of the Father in my name, he may give it you. 17 These things I command you, that ye love one another.

How will you know a disciple of Christ?
You will know them by their love.

KJV... John 13: 34-35

34 A new commandment I give unto you, That ye love one another; as I have loved you, that ye also love one another. 35 By this shall all men know that ye are my disciples, if ye have love one to another.

It is necessary to obey God above men.

KJV.... Acts 5: 29-32

29 Then Peter and the other apostles answered and said, We ought to obey God rather than men. 30 The God of our fathers raised up Jesus, whom ye slew and hanged on a tree. 31 Him hath God exalted with his right hand to be a Prince and a Saviour, for to give repentance to Israel, and forgiveness of sins. 32 And we are his witnesses of these things; and so is also the Holy Ghost, whom God hath given to them that obey him.

11.4. Ready to Discern and Receive.

One must pay attention to the voice of the Holy Spirit. The children of God have the ability through God to discern what is happening during moments of deliverance.

KJV....1 John 5:1-5

Whosoever believeth that Jesus is the Christ is born of God: and every one that loveth him that begat loveth him also that is begotten of him. 2 By this we know that we love the children of God, when we love God, and keep his commandments. 3 For this is the love of God, that we keep his commandments: and his commandments are not grievous. 4 For whatsoever is born of God overcometh the world: and this is the victory that overcometh the world, even our faith. 5 Who is he that overcometh the world, but he that believeth that Jesus is the Son of God?

Let every soul be subject unto the higher powers. For there is no power but of God: the powers that be are ordained of God.

11.5. An Active Member of the Body of Christ submitted to authority.

A person should be an active member of the body of Christ and be willing to submit to authority. Those who do not understand the power do not have the base for understanding and certainty they need to subject demons to the obedience of Christ and his Word. Their life is in conflict with the principles established by God for man. If they are not willing to subject to authority, then they are disobedient, and this condition shows that they do not have the calling for this ministry. Their subjugation, binding, and obedience must attest to the authority that they will use to control demons in the same way.

KJV... Romans 13:1- 10

Let every soul be subject unto the higher powers. For there is no power but of God: the powers that be are ordained of God. 2 Whosoever therefore resisteth the power, resisteth the ordinance of God: and they that resist shall receive to themselves damnation. 3 For rulers are not a terror to good works, but to the evil. Wilt thou then not be afraid of the power? do that which is good, and thou shalt have praise of the same: 4 For he is the minister of God to thee for good. But if thou do that which is evil, be afraid; for he beareth not the sword in vain: for he is the minister of God, a revenger to execute wrath upon him that doeth evil. 5 Wherefore ye must needs be subject, not only for wrath, but also for conscience sake. 6 For for this cause pay ye tribute also: for they are God's ministers, attending continually upon this very thing. 7 Render therefore to all their dues: tribute to whom tribute is due; custom to whom custom; fear to whom fear; honour to whom honour. 8 Owe no man any thing, but to love one another: for he that loveth another hath fulfilled the law 9 For this, Thou shalt not commit adultery, Thou shalt not kill, Thou shalt not steal, Thou shalt not bear false witness, Thou shalt not covet; and if there be any other commandment, it is briefly comprehended in this saying, namely, Thou shalt love thy neighbour as thyself. 10 Love worketh no ill to his neighbour: therefore love is the fulfilling of the law.

11.6. Understand the Word of God.

The word of God is the sword of defense in spiritual warfare. Unleashing this weapon is the order that one must obey, and all creation submits to it.

Scripture gives us an understanding of how we are to remain within the will of God

> **KJV....John 8.31-32**
>
> *31 Then said Jesus to those Jews which believed on him, If ye continue in my word, then are ye my disciples indeed;*
>
> *32 And ye shall know the truth, and the truth shall make you free.*

Scripture is needed for our correction and instruction.

> **KJV.... John 5: 39**
>
> *39 Search the scriptures; for in them ye think ye have eternal life: and they are they which testify of me.*
>
> **KJV....2 Timothy 3:14-17**
>
> *14 But continue thou in the things which thou hast learned and hast been assured of, knowing of whom thou hast learned them; 15 And that from a child thou hast known the holy scriptures, which are able to make thee wise unto salvation through faith which is in Christ Jesus. 16 All scripture is given by inspiration of God, and is profitable for doctrine, for reproof, for correction,*

for instruction in righteousness: 17 That the man of God may be perfect, thoroughly furnished unto all good works.

Unadulterated spiritual milk means that we receive direct revelation from the teacher without intermediaries. This happens through the Holy Spirit and is for our personal edification. It comes directly from God.

> *So that the man of God may be thoroughly equipped for every good work*

KJV....1 Peter 2:1-5

But there were false prophets also among the people, even as there shall be false teachers among you, who privily shall bring in damnable heresies, even denying the Lord that bought them, and bring upon themselves swift destruction. 2 And many shall follow their pernicious ways; by reason of whom the way of truth shall be evil spoken of. 3 And through covetousness shall they with feigned words make merchandise of you: whose judgment now of a long time lingereth not, and their damnation slumbereth not. 4 For if God spared not the angels that sinned, but cast them down to hell, and delivered them into chains of darkness, to be reserved unto judgment; 5 And spared not the old world, but saved Noah the eighth person, a preacher of righteousness, bringing in the flood upon the world of the ungodly;

11.7. Search for Holiness.

To identify a committed Christian, we must look at their testimony and see the fruit of the Spirit reflected in them.

KJV... 1 John 3: 6-9

6 Whosoever abideth in him sinneth not: whosoever sinneth hath not seen him, neither known him. 7 Little children, let no man deceive you: he that doeth righteousness is righteous, even as he is righteous. 8 He that committeth sin is of the devil; for the devil sinneth from the beginning. For this purpose the Son of God was manifested, that he might destroy the works of the devil. 9 Whosoever is born of God doth not commit sin; for his seed remaineth in him: and he cannot sin, because he is born of God.

To be imitators of Christ means that we do the same as Christ did in his Ministry and in the dedication and love he displayed, eventually give your life.

1 Peter 1:13-16

13 Wherefore gird up the loins of your mind, be sober, and hope to the end for the grace that is to be brought unto you at the revelation of Jesus Christ; 14 As obedient children, not fashioning yourselves according to the former lusts in your ignorance: 15 But as he which hath called you is holy, so be ye holy in all manner of conversation; 16 Because it is written, Be ye holy; for I am holy.

Living conformed to the Spirit and not conformed to the flesh, God gives us the ability to overcome every test.

KJV... Romans 8: 6-16

6 For to be carnally minded is death; but to be spiritually minded is life and peace. 7 Because the carnal mind is enmity against God: for it is not subject to the law of God, neither indeed can be. 8 So then they that are in the flesh cannot please God. 9 But ye are not in the flesh, but in the Spirit, if so be that the Spirit of God dwell in you. Now if any man have not the Spirit of Christ, he is none of his. 10 And if Christ be in you, the body is dead because of sin; but the Spirit is life because of righteousness. 11 But if the Spirit of him that raised up Jesus from the dead dwell in you, he that raised up Christ from the dead shall also quicken your mortal bodies by his Spirit that dwelleth in you. 12 Therefore, brethren, we are debtors, not to the flesh, to live after the flesh. 13 For if ye live after the flesh, ye shall die: but if ye through the Spirit do mortify the deeds of the body, ye shall live. 14 For as many as are led by the Spirit of God, they are the sons of God. 15 For ye have not received the spirit of bondage again to fear; but ye have received the Spirit of adoption, whereby we cry, Abba, Father. 16 The Spirit itself beareth witness with our spirit, that we are the children of God:

11.8. Have a Calling to the Service.

I feel that I had this calling through my experiences with self-deliverance. God himself chose me. Only the person themselves can know and feel if they have this calling. That was my personal experience.

When God calls us to service, we are filled with the Spirit which gives us wisdom, intelligence, and knowledge to do what we are called to do.

KJV... Exodus 31 1:6

And the Lord spake unto Moses, saying, 2 See, I have called by name Bezaleel the son of Uri, the son of Hur, of the tribe of Judah: 3 And I have filled him with the spirit of God, in wisdom, and in understanding, and in knowledge, and in all manner of workmanship, 4 To devise cunning works, to work in gold, and in silver, and in brass, 5 And in cutting of stones, to set them, and in carving of timber, to work in all manner of workmanship. 6 And I, behold, I have given with him Aholiab, the son of Ahisamach, of the tribe of Dan: and in the hearts of all that are wise hearted I have put wisdom, that they may make all that I have commanded thee;

God will not take away the gift or the calling that he has given you. Therefore, if you have it and it is known in your heart that it is true, then there is no reason to doubt.

I have filled you with the Spirit which gives us wisdom, intelligence, and knowledge.

KJV... Romans 11:29

29 For the gifts and calling of God are without repentance.

The purpose of call is to ensure that we do not doubt our service, and so we know that it is God's will for our lives.

KJV... Romans 8:28 -37

28 And we know that all things work together for good to them that love God, to them who are the called according to his purpose. 29 For whom he did foreknow, he also did predestinate to be conformed to the image of his Son, that he might be the firstborn among many brethren. 30 Moreover whom he did predestinate, them he also called: and whom he called, them he also justified: and whom he justified, them he also glorified. 31 What shall we then say to these things? If God be for us, who can be against us? 32 He that spared not his own Son, but delivered him up for us all, how shall he not with him also freely give us all things? 33 Who shall lay any thing to the charge of God's elect? It is God that justifieth. 34 Who is he that condemneth? It is Christ that died, yea rather, that is risen again, who is even at the right hand of God, who also maketh intercession for us. 35 Who shall separate us from the love of Christ? shall tribulation, or distress, or persecution, or famine, or nakedness, or peril, or sword? 36 As it is written, For thy sake we are killed all the day long; we are accounted as sheep for the slaughter. 37 Nay, in all these things we are more than conquerors through him that loved us.

11.9. Unquestioned Integrity.

The things that a child of light does stay on the light and nothing can hide them, not even if he is ashamed.

KJV...1 Timothy 3:8-13

8 Likewise must the deacons be grave, not doubletongued, not given to much wine, not greedy of filthy lucre; 9 Holding the mystery of the faith in a pure conscience. 10 And let these also first be proved; then let them use the office of a deacon, being found blameless. 11 Even so must their wives be grave, not slanderers, sober, faithful in all things. 12 Let the deacons be the husbands of one wife, ruling their children and their own houses well. 13 For they that have used the office of a deacon well purchase to themselves a good degree, and great boldness in the faith which is in Christ Jesus.

We are no longer what we were when we had our old nature. However, we are accustomed of living in a way that allows us to have our old behaviors. The new nature is to take over and give us what we need to resist the devil so that we will flee from circumstances that can lead us to fall.

11.10. Humility.

Humility was an attribute of Jesus and should be reflected in the children of God given through his superiority, when He took the form of man, He did not consider himself to be equal to God. He gave up his life as a deity because of his love and obedience.

> **KJV.... Phillipians 2: 2-11**
>
> *2 Fulfil ye my joy, that ye be likeminded, having the same love, being of one accord, of one mind. 3 Let nothing be done through strife or vainglory; but in lowliness of mind let each esteem other better than themselves. 4 Look not every man on his own things, but every man also on the things of others. 5 Let this mind be in you, which was also in Christ Jesus: 6 Who, being in the form of God, thought it not robbery to be equal with God: 7 But made himself of no reputation, and took upon him the form of a servant, and was made in the likeness of men: 8 And being found in fashion as a man, he humbled himself, and became obedient unto death, even the death of the cross. 9 Wherefore God also hath highly exalted him, and given him a name which is above every name: 10 That at the name of Jesus every knee should bow, of things in heaven, and things in earth, and things under the earth; 11 And that every tongue should confess that Jesus Christ is Lord, to the glory of God the Father.*

Paul said that there is nothing better to glorify ourselves with than our weakness because it is there that God shows brightest. What God wants will happen, but not everything that happens is because God wants it.

KJV. 2 Corinthians 12:1-12

It is not expedient for me doubtless to glory. I will come to visions and revelations of the Lord. 2 I knew a man in Christ above fourteen years ago, (whether in the body, I cannot tell; or whether out of the body, I cannot tell: God knoweth;) such an one caught up to the third heaven. 3 And I knew such a man, (whether in the body, or out of the body, I cannot tell: God knoweth;) 4 How that he was caught up into paradise, and heard unspeakable words, which it is not lawful for a man to utter. 5 Of such an one will I glory: yet of myself I will not glory, but in mine infirmities. 6 For though I would desire to glory, I shall not be a fool; for I will say the truth: but now I forbear, lest any man should think of me above that which he seeth me to be, or that he heareth of me. 7 And lest I should be exalted above measure through the abundance of the revelations, there was given to me a thorn in the flesh, the messenger of Satan to buffet me, lest I should be exalted above measure. 8 For this thing I besought the Lord thrice, that it might depart from me. 9 And he said unto me, My grace is sufficient for thee: for my strength is made perfect in weakness. Most gladly therefore will I rather glory in my infirmities, that the power of Christ may rest upon me. 10 Therefore I take pleasure in infirmities, in reproaches, in necessities, in persecutions, in distresses for Christ's sake: for when I am weak, then am I strong. 11 I am become a fool in glorying; ye have compelled me: for I ought to have been commended of you: for in nothing am I behind the very chiefest apostles, though I be nothing. 12 Truly the signs of an apostle

> ***And being in the condition of man, humbled himself, becoming obedient to death and death on a cross***

were wrought among you in all patience, in signs, and wonders, and mighty deeds

11.11. Compassion.

It is necessary to have a genuine love, to desire with a genuine heart to free the children of God. It should not be done for money or because of vanity. It must be acknowledged that this is not of you, but that it comes from God and that it is a privilege to be an instrument of God used to give freedom.

KJV.... Colossians 3:12-21

12 Put on therefore, as the elect of God, holy and beloved, bowels of mercies, kindness, humbleness of mind, meekness, longsuffering; 13 Forbearing one another, and forgiving one another, if any man have a quarrel against any: even as Christ forgave you, so also do ye. 14 And above all these things put on charity, which is the bond of perfectness. 15 And let the peace of God rule in your hearts, to the which also ye are called in one body; and be ye thankful. 16 Let the word of Christ dwell in you richly in all wisdom; teaching and admonishing one another in psalms and hymns and spiritual songs, singing with grace in your hearts to the Lord. 17 And whatsoever ye do in word or deed, do all in the name of the Lord Jesus, giving thanks to God and the Father by him. 18 Wives, submit yourselves unto your own husbands, as it is fit in the Lord. 19 Husbands, love your wives, and be not bitter against them. 20 Children, obey your parents in all things: for this is well pleasing unto the Lord. 21 Fathers, provoke not your children to anger, lest they be discouraged.

11.12. Confidentiality and Trustworthiness.

Prudence, discretion, and confidentiality are important parts of this ministry which is founded on trust. It is important to understand that you are not allowed to divulge or expose in public the information that you have been given from people whom you have freed. However, with the permission of the person, a testimony can be published in order to glorify God, but it should not question, call out, or judge the sinner.

11.13. Security and Conviction of the Power granted through Jesus and the order to faithfully complete the required work.

At the beginning of his ministry, Jesus sent out his disciples and granted them power over evil spirits. He also ordered them to go only to the Jews and not the Gentiles, and we should note that this order included Judas Iscariot. This power is the Holy Spirit, and as we know, Satan still entered him.

> *He gave them power against unclean spirits, to cast them out, and to heal all manner of sickness and all manner of disease.*

KJV...Matthew 10: 1

And when he had called unto him his twelve disciples, he gave them power against unclean spirits, to cast them out, and to heal all manner of sickness and all manner of disease.

This ministry was originally for the lost sheep of Israel.

KJV...Matthew 10: 5-8

⁵ These twelve Jesus sent forth, and commanded them, saying, Go not into the way of the Gentiles, and into any city of the Samaritans enter ye not: 6 But go rather to the lost sheep of the house of Israel. 7 And as ye go, preach, saying, The kingdom of heaven is at hand. 8 Heal the sick, cleanse the lepers, raise the dead, cast out devils: freely ye have received, freely give.

Jesus sent out the disciples in groups of two and gave them the authority over evil spirits.

KJV...Marks 6:7-13

⁷ And he called unto him the twelve, and began to send them forth by two and two; and gave them power over unclean spirits; 8 And commanded them that they should take nothing for their journey, save a staff only; no scrip, no bread, no money in their purse: 9 But be shod with sandals; and not put on two coats. 10 And he said unto them, In what place soever ye enter into an house, there abide till ye depart from that place. 11 And whosoever shall not receive you, nor hear you, when ye depart thence, shake off the dust under your feet for a testimony against them. Verily I say unto you, It shall be more tolerable for Sodom and Gomorrha in the day of judgment, than for that city. 12 And they went out, and preached that men should

> **Then saith he unto his disciples, The harvest truly is plenteous, but the labourers are few; Pray ye therefore the Lord of the harvest, that he will send forth labourers into his harvest.**

repent. 13 And they cast out many devils, and anointed with oil many that were sick, and healed them.

Jesus also chose seventy more people and sent them out with authority, telling them to beg for more workers.

KJV...Luke 10:1-2

After these things the Lord appointed other seventy also, and sent them two and two before his face into every city and place, whither he himself would come. 2 Therefore said he unto them, The harvest truly is great, but the labourers are few: pray ye therefore the Lord of the harvest, that he would send forth labourers into his harvest.

These seventy-two reported great results from their missions.

KJV.... Luke 10:16-20

16 He that heareth you heareth me; and he that despiseth you despiseth me; and he that despiseth me despiseth him that sent me. 17 And the seventy returned again with joy, saying, Lord, even the devils are subject unto us through thy name. 18 And he said unto them, I beheld Satan as lightning fall from heaven. 19 Behold, I give unto you power to tread on serpents and scorpions, and over all the power of the enemy: and nothing shall by any means hurt you. 20 Notwithstanding in this rejoice not, that the spirits are subject unto you; but rather rejoice, because your names are written in heaven.

The sin of Jews as they rejected Jesus allowed God to extend salvation to the Gentiles in order to make his people jealous. Because of this, Paul was charged with extending the kingdom to us, the Gentiles, with the same instructions and orders that he received from Jesus.

KJV... Romans 11 2-14

2 God hath not cast away his people which he foreknew. Wot ye not what the scripture saith of Elias? how he maketh intercession to God against Israel saying, 3 Lord, they have killed thy prophets, and digged down thine altars; and I am left alone, and they seek my life. 4 But what saith the answer of God unto him? I have reserved to myself seven thousand men, who have not bowed the knee to the image of Baal. 5 Even so then at this present time also there is a remnant according to the election of grace. 6 And if by grace, then is it no more of works: otherwise grace is no more grace. But if it be of works, then it is no more grace: otherwise work is no more work. 7 What then? Israel hath not obtained that which he seeketh for; but the election hath obtained it, and the rest were blinded. 8 (According as it is written, God hath given them the spirit of slumber, eyes that they should not see, and ears that they should not hear;) unto this day. 9 And David saith, Let their table be made a snare, and a trap, and a stumblingblock, and a recompence unto them: 10 Let their eyes be darkened, that they may not see, and bow down their back alway. 11 I say then, Have they stumbled that they should fall? God forbid: but rather through their fall salvation is come unto the Gentiles, for to provoke them to jealousy. 12 Now if the fall of them be the riches of the world, and the diminishing of them the riches of the Gentiles; how much more their fulness? 13 For I speak to you Gentiles, inasmuch as I am the apostle of the Gentiles, I magnify mine office: 14 If by any means I may provoke to emulation them which are my flesh, and might save some of them.

Jesus himself sent out the disciples so that they would disciple others and told them to keep track of everything that had been entrusted to them. Through them, we have the same charge.

KJV.... Matthew 28 16-20

16 Then the eleven disciples went away into Galilee, into a mountain where Jesus had appointed them. 17 And when they saw him, they worshipped him: but some doubted. 18 And Jesus came and spake unto them, saying, All power is given unto me in heaven and in earth. 19 Go ye therefore, and teach all nations, baptizing them in the name of the Father, and of the Son, and of the Holy Ghost: 20 Teaching them to observe all things whatsoever I have commanded you: and, lo, I am with you always, even unto the end of the world. Amen.

Paul himself took the gospel of Christ to the Gentiles.

Acts 22:17-21

17 And it came to pass, that, when I was come again to Jerusalem, even while I prayed in the temple, I was in a trance; 18 And saw him saying unto me, Make haste, and get thee quickly out of Jerusalem: for they will not receive thy testimony concerning me. 19 And I said, Lord, they know that I imprisoned and beat in every synagogue them that believed on thee: 20 And when the blood of thy martyr Stephen was shed, I also was standing by, and consenting unto his death, and kept the raiment of them that slew him. 21 And he said unto me, Depart: for I will send thee far hence unto the Gentiles.

By the instruction of Paul, the disciple, He tells us to be imitators of Christ. Not to judge anyone for anything and to guard our hearts. Paul himself was an imitator of Jesus.

11.14. Spiritual, Emotional, and Physical Training, Wisdom, and Complete Peace.

Spiritual Training. In holiness, prayer, and faith.
Training in Wisdom and Knowledge.
With the fear of the Lord, acknowledging his absolute authority and power. With understanding of his Word, the power that he gives to his ministries, and the power of the Word as a sword.

Physical. Because of the time and energy that will be spend, they must remain calm, without striving or tiring out. They must have time to commit to the work and not leave things undone. They should sleep, eat well, and stay active.

Emotional. Firmly acknowledge that they are God's and that the work they do for Him is: understand the importance of their part in the ministry as something that God supports as His own.

We should never be striving, we should be in complete peace. God is always in control.

> *His absolute authority and power, with the knowledge of his word, power delegated in his ministers, and the power of his word as a sword.*

KJV....1 Corinthians 2:9-15

9 But as it is written, Eye hath not seen, nor ear heard, neither have entered into the heart of man, the things which God hath prepared for them that love him. 10 But God hath revealed them unto us by his Spirit: for the Spirit searcheth all things, yea, the deep things of God. 11 For what man knoweth the things of a man, save the spirit of man which is in him? even so the things of God knoweth no man, but the Spirit of God. 12 Now we have received, not the spirit of the world, but the spirit which is of God; that we might know the things that are freely given to us of God. 13 Which things also we speak, not in the words which man's wisdom teacheth, but which the Holy Ghost teacheth; comparing spiritual things with spiritual. 14 But the natural man receiveth not the things of the Spirit of God: for they are foolishness unto him: neither can he know them, because they are spiritually discerned. 15 But he that is spiritual judgeth all things, yet he himself is judged of no man.

> **For the word of God is quick, and powerful, and sharper than any twoedged sword, piercing even to the dividing asunder of soul and spirit, and of the joints and marrow, and is a discerner of the thoughts and intents of the heart**

Acknowledging the power of the Word and the power of the new condition that we have as children through the Blood of Jesus.

KJV....Hebrews 4:12

12 For the word of God is quick, and powerful, and sharper than any twoedged sword, piercing even to the dividing asunder of soul and spirit, and of the joints and marrow, and is a discerner of the thoughts and intents of the heart.

Believe in the power of the Blood of Christ. My faith is the main instrument of the ministry.

KJV... Matthew 17:15-21

15 Lord, have mercy on my son: for he is lunatick, and sore vexed: for ofttimes he falleth into the fire, and oft into the water. 16 And I brought him to thy disciples, and they could not cure him. 17 Then Jesus answered and said, O faithless and perverse generation, how long shall I be with you? how long shall I suffer you? bring him hither to me. 18 And Jesus rebuked the devil; and he departed out of him: and the child was cured from that very hour. 19 Then came the disciples to Jesus apart, and said, Why could not we cast him out? 20 And Jesus said unto them, Because of your unbelief: for verily I say unto you, If ye have faith as a grain of mustard seed, ye shall say unto this mountain, Remove hence to yonder place; and it shall remove; and nothing shall be impossible unto you. 21 Howbeit this kind goeth not out but by prayer and fasting.

11.15. Have No Fear, Recognize the Authority that has been given for this Service.

They should have no fear since they completely trust and understand that he who is in me is greater than the one who is the world.

2 Timothy 1:7.

⁷ For God hath not given us the spirit of fear; but of power, and of love, and of a sound mind.

> *For God hath not given us the spirit of fear; but of power, and of love, and of a sound mind.*

11.16. Benefits of having a Deliverance Team.

We will be completing the Great Commission in its entirety.

Yes, this is part of the Great Commission that has often been left out. Cast out demons. Set the captives free. This ministry wholly addresses the Great Commission and does not leave it half-done as the majority of churches do. That is exactly what this book aims to do; equip the people of God!

John 14:12

Verily, verily, I say unto you, He that believeth on me, the works that I do shall he do also; and greater works than these shall he do; because I go unto my Father.

John 20:21

²¹ Then said Jesus to them again, Peace be unto you: as my Father hath sent me, even so send I you.

Members will not leave to look for help somewhere else.

This is what happens right now. Many hopeless people come to our ministry looking for help. One of the goals of this book is to give you as a pastor or leader the skills for Deliverance so that you can attend to the sheep of the Lord that he has asked you to care for and to heal.

A Congregation Free of Demons.

This is the great blessing! Freedom from demonic oppression.

A Congregation that is physically and Spiritually Clean.

Yes, to be free of demonic oppression is what Jesus wants for us. We have the power and authority from God on our side. .

Living by signs and preaching.

If the teachings of this book are put into practice, there is a high probability that those who come will experience an explosion of life because of the signs and teaching they will be given.

Acts 5:16

[16] There also came a multitude out of the cities round about unto Jerusalem, bringing sick folks, and them which were vexed with unclean spirits: and they were healed every one.

11.17. Duties of the members.

Have Passed through Deliverance.

There is no exception here. Everyone who is part of the ministry team must have gone through the process of deliverance first.

Have a calling to this Ministry. .

I feel that I have been called to my experiences of self-deliverance. God prepared me himself. Only the person can know it and feel it.

Have a Healthy Marriage.

It is preferable if you are married. Your spouse can help you when you are attacked in by demons in retaliation. My wife has been a huge help.

Be Willing to Die.

When I say die, it is truly to die; to be put to death for the sake of Christ by entering into battle with demons. However, remember that they cannot take our lives.

> *Your spouse can help you when you are attacked in by demons in retaliation. My wife has been a huge help.*

Have Personal Deliverance Experience.

This is key. The Holy Spirit must train you through personal attacks in your life. This was my experience.

Learn how to release yourself.

You should seriously prepare yourself to learn how to self-deliverance as soon as possible. You could be alone when you experience an attack. This happens to me daily. I am constantly liberating myself.

Have women on your team.

> Especially when a woman is in need of deliverance. We must be careful not to open any doors to Satan.

Who should choose.

> The Holy Spirit. There should be an appeal made to those who feel as if they have been. This is the important question. Who feels that God has called them to the Deliverance mimistry. That is how it should be.

Study this topic.

> They should acquire good books. There are many good books on this subject, and of course you should have all of our books in your library. Study them many times. We have published several books from everything that we are experiencing in our Deliverance ministry, Cristo Libera.

Stay in Groups of two or three.

> There should be no more than two or three people in each group with one leader in each. Depending on the size of the congregation and the demonic oppression, there could be several teams.
> **OTHERS:**
> Those that God reveals.

You should seriously prepare yourself to learn how to self-deliverance as soon as possible. You could be alone when you experience an attack. This happens to me daily. I am constantly liberating myself.

11.18. Key Duties for those who are to be deliveranced.

Preparation is very helpful when receiving deliverance. For example, forgiving others, asking forgiveness, refraining from sin, fasting for at least three days, and reading books on deliverance are key to being set free. If you learn about deliverance, it is much easier to be freed and to stay that way. You should do this daily. It is a daily work that keeps us from sin because Satan walks like a Lion seeking those whom he can devour. If we are careless, we can again let demons in. If a free person learns about deliverance, then they can also help others to be free. This is one of the goals of this book; that people of God would rise in thanks for what Christ has done for us, Warriors, an army of people serving the Church that has been bought by the Blood!

11.19. How much time does deliverance take?

This varies, but it is recommended that you set aside 2 or 3 hours. It can be very tiring for both the deliverance team and the individual. Sometimes it is necessary to bind the spirits, take a break, and come back for another round. You should repeat the steps, praying, fasting, remembering old sin, confessing, etc.

11.20. How do you support this ministry?

Praying, incredible amounts of praying are required. If it is possible, the ministry should be included in the praying of the church because it is very important to the congregation. This is the way to ward of following attacks.

11.21. Where to do deliverance.

- I. It should be in a hidden room, and you should be anointed with oil if possible.
- II. Furnished. Everyone should be able to sit. It could last several hours, and we want to avoid wearing any out physically.
- III. Cleaning paper or toilet paper rolls.
- IV. Water to drink and to clean up in case there is vomit.
- V. Garbage bins and plastic bags.
- VI. Pencils, notebooks. This is if you want to take notes and keep a personal record of people who have been freed, the names of demons, etc.

11.22. The process of deliverance.

- I. Contact the team.
- II. If it is possible, read at least one book about deliverance. One of ours or some other one. Become familiar with deliverance. That is the goal.
- III. Fill in the form for deliverance.
- IV. Confess sins.
- V. Forgive and ask forgiveness.
- VI. Make an appointment.

11.23. The day is here! The hour of deliverance!

I'll explain how we normally do them. You can make changes if you'd like. We are all guided by the Holy Spirit. Before the appointment, the person should fill out the form (it is in the book), and renounce their sins. This is assuming they have already settled their life with Christ, with others, and with themselves.

The expected moment is finally here! Moreover, the person who is being deliveranced; nervously and uncertainty. This is why I usually ask everyone to kneel in the room for 15 or 30 minutes remembering and confession their sins to Jesus. After, we pray and cast out any demon that has already been seen in the room.

11.24. Ask the Holy Spirit to guide us.

We pray for protection. We cloth ourselves with the Armor of God and cover ourselves with the Blood of Jesus. We also cover our families and properties and ask the Holy Spirit to guide us.

After we all sit down with the questionnaire in our hands, we ask them to close their eyes so as not to be distracted.

I begin to cast out demons immediately, generational ones, those from their sin. I destroy curses and pacts and I remove everything including sickness. (All of these prayers are in the second book.) We are guided by revelations from the Holy Spirit and by the questionnaire. After we finish everything, if the person has been freed, then we take a short 3 to 6 minute break, and I start a second kind of ministring.

I order, always in the Name the Christ, that any demon related to this person present itself, especially those with the most power; the boss. If nothing comes from this, it is because the person was freed through the first ministry, and we pray. We give thanks to God for everything, and we go home. But if a demon does present itself, then we begin to ask questions about its name, how many there are, what harm it is causing, where the demons are, if they are on the wife, or kids..., etc.

For each response that we get from a demon, we always ask it if what has been said can be proven before the Throne of Jehovah God. This is so that we are tricked because they often lie. After this, we cast them out. Here we must be guided by the

> *For each response that we get from a demon, we always ask it if what has been said can be proven before the Throne of Jehovah God.*

Holy Spirit. Then we go from kingdom to kingdom, repeating the process until there is nothing left. If there is any resistance, we ask what legal right the demon has and show it that the right has been removed by Christ on the Cross through his Blood. We are adamant about this. (See the testimonies and processes in this book)

Once we have cast all of them out and give thanks to God, give them sentences that are written in this book to keep his release. We have more prayers in our Book Manual: freedom, so that the person can stay free. Then we clean up and head home!

THINGS TO REMEMBER
Continued

- *If you abide in my Word, you are truly my disciples, and you will know the truth and the truth shall make you free.*

- *As obedient children, do not be conformed to your prior desire that controlled you because of your ignorance.*

- *Deacons also must be honest, without bending.*

- *Therefore, undoing the lie, speak honestly with your neighbor, for we are all members of one another.*

- *Therefore, for the sake of Christ I rejoice in weaknesses, insults, persecution, woes; when I am weak, then I am strong.*

- *For verily I say unto you that everything you bind on earth shall be bound in heaven; and everything you loose on Earth will be loosed in heaven.*

as I have kept my Father's commandments, and abide in his love.

- *In this we know that we love the children of God, when we love God and keep his commandments.*

12.
HOW TO DESTROY THE MOST COMMON WITCHCRAFT

Witchcraft consists of curses, spells, conjurations, or other words. They are sent through objects or in other forms to a person or an animal. Those who carry out the curses are demons. In my experience in the work of deliverance, I've encountered many people who have been cursed. Approximately 98% of all followers of Christ who have been freed by this Ministry of Freedom and Health. They had been cursed by witchcraft. The practice of the occult is very common.

    Many people use this method, instead of a gun. To cause damage to others. They search for a person that knows how to make spells and curses. The most common curses I've encountered are those cast through dolls, photographs, food, drinks, clothing, perfumes, powders, pacts, cemetery ground, dedications, animal sacrifices.

    Therefore, we must be very careful. A Christian cannot be cursed because God has already cleansed him, but they can try to curse him by these things. The demon cannot enter, but it will stay close, circling the Christian. If you open the doors to sin. This curse or spell will enter. The demon will follow through in the order it was given. See the testimonies and deliverance process further on in this book.

All curses and witchcraft can be canceled out and broken through Jesus Christ.

To continue, I'll present the prayers and forms that I use to free people from curses. I suggest that if you know or suspect whomever it was that made or said the curse, then you should focus the prayer toward them, be specific and declare it with FAITH.

12.1. Witchcraft from pictures or dolls with pins or needles.

This is very common. In all of my large campaigns and personal deliverance; I destroy, in the Name of Jesus, the Witchcraft made in this manner. People feel it when the needles are removed.

Testimonies.

I remember a family member who suffered from pains and was often taken to the emergency room. She did not believe much in the deliverance until she had witnessed a few of them in person. On the last day of the campaign, after two months, she decided to accept a scan (that is what I call it) to see if there was anything there. She was crying in fear and pain when I started to break the curses and remove the needles. She felt them coming out of her arms, her head, and her face, everywhere. Thanks to Jesus Christ, she was freed and from that moment all of her pains and sicknesses stopped. They had been witchcraft. I stayed in contact with her, and she told me that since then, she has not had any migraines or pains. Glory to Jesus!

Almost always, after I do a mass deliverance at a church. Many people come up to me and say they could feel it when the needles were removed from their bodies and their discomfort stopped after the Witchcraft from needles had been destroyed. You can find these testimonies on my website www.cristolibera.org.

Prayer to destroy Witchcraft from pictures or dolls with pins.

In the Name of Jesus, I send the sword that is the Word of God to wherever these photos and dolls are. I take hold of them and move them to the clean and Holy place. In the Name of Jesus, I remove all of the needles and pins from their heads, throats, mouths, backs, arms, chest, hearts, stomachs, private parts, knees, legs, hands, and all of the body. Don't leave a single needle. DONE! DON'T LEAVE A SINGLE NEEDLE!

Now, in the Name of Jesus, I remove all of the bonds, chains, cemetery earth, or anything that has been placed on top of it. Right now, in the NAME OF JESUS, I cancel all of the spells, curses, and evil words that have been spoken. DONE, I DECLARE IT ALL VOID!

Now, in the Name of Jesus, I bless this photo or doll. In the name of Jesus, I cancel, break and undo everything this doll or photo has to do with you or any person. THIS Witchcraft IS BROKEN AND CANCELLED! Demons from Witchcraft, all is done. NOW IN THE NAME OF JESUS, GET OUT, YOU NO LONGER HAVE A LEGAL RIGHT, GET OUT!

12.2. Witchcraft from food or drink.

This is also very common. If you suspect someone, don't accept anything from them.

Testimony: I heard about the case of Elvira (name has been changed) who was sick for 12 years. She had blotches all over her body, feet full of blood and cuts on her feet. This woman had to sleep on the floor because she could not stay in bed. Her husband had to carry her on his back.

Once I heard about this, I immediately called her on the phone. She lived in another country, and as you know I live in the US. However, for God, nothing is impossible, and distance does not matter. In the process of deliverance, the demon was discovered, and it confessed. It said its name was Maria Lionza, a demon that is well known in Venezuela, and it was there because of a curse. It had been sent through passion fruit juice that Elvira's neighbor had given her, and she drank. The sickness and destruction began after she drank it.

Fortunately, Elvira is a Christian, and she was able to be set free from this demon and the sickness.

Prayer to break Witchcraft from food or drink.

GLORY TO JESUS CHRIST THROUGH WHOM WE HAVE BLESSING AND TOTAL FREEDOM!

IN THE NAME OF JESUS! I break and cancel all curses, spells, and evil words that have been sent through food or drink and that I (whichever person) have taken in.

DONE! I BREAK IT ALL! Now in the name of Jesus, I bless this food and drink.

DONE! I BREAK AND CANCEL THIS Witchcraft!

Therefore, demons from curses get out, get out. You do not have any legal right or permission to be here.

I send you into the abyss in the name of Jesus. *OUT, OUT IN THE NAME OF JESUS!*

12.3. Witchcraft from clothing, nails, hair, body parts, perfumes, powders, or names.

These are also very common. You must be very careful with presents, especially those that we make, walk on, lose or lend out. I have seen many people cursed through these practices.

Testimonies.

As you know, I have thousands of videos on deliverance on the Internet from the people who are in touch through this ministry. One of these people was a young girl from Mexico named Rosalba. She told me her tragic story, her story of suffering. In 6 years, she had tried to commit suicide seven times. On time, she took more than 90 antidepressant pills and slit her veins. In her Internet account, she told me that she had lost lots of intimate apparel, and when she told me this, I saw how she had come into all of this evil. I suggested that we do a small deliverance and in a day or so, we would continue.

She accepted immediately. The first and only thing I did that day was cancel the Witchcraft from clothing that were on her. Automatically the demons from curses manifested and left through vomiting. She was free! GLORY TO JESUS CHRIST! Her face changed and then she became hungry. Later, we continued with more deliverances.

Pray.

In the name of Jesus I cancel and break all curses, spells, and evil words that have been placed on clothing, nails, hair, and parts of the body, perfumes, powders, or names. ALL IS DONE WITH THESE DEMONS FROM Witchcraft. OUT IN THE NAME OF JESUS. GET OUT, OUT!

12.4. Witchcraft from blood pacts or other demonic pacts.

Curses from pacts made through the blood of humans or animal sacrifices. These are also very common and can be placed even before someone is born. They are born with the demon from whichever pact has been placed on their ancestors. Because of this, it is very important to do a deep deliverance.

Testimonies of deliverance from Pacts.

I'll tell you the most recent deliverance that I encountered of this kind. This person had a pact made by its own father since his father was not Christian and had been practicing witchcraft. Thanks God the demon confessed why it would not leave and we confronted it with the Pact of the Blood of Jesus. Which they are very familiar with, and in this way the person was set free from the evil spirit.

Pray

IN THE NAME OF JESUS, I cancel all the demonic pacts that have been made through animal sacrifices, cats, dogs, people or whichever animal and pacts of all form. All has been canceled by the pact of the Blood of Jesus Christ that was made on the Cross at the Calvary. This pact of the Blood of Jesus Christ is more powerful than all satanic pacts and, therefore, all are annulled before the Pact of Jesus. Therefore, GET OUT in the NAME OF JESUS, get out, out! You have no legal right or permission to stay. Out in the name of Jesus!

Pray to break Witchcraft in all forms.

This prayer is made in the end. In case there are any other curse that need to be broken.

IN THE NAME OF JESUS, I BREAK, CANCEL, AND UNDO ALL CURSES, SPELLS, CONJURATIONS, DAMNATIONS, blood rituals, prayers, or witchcraft THAT HAS BEEN MADE AGAINST ME OR (NAME).

EVERYTHING IS CANCELLED AND BROKEN! Now demons from witchcraft, GET OUT! You have no legal right or permission to be in me, I break this curse. YOUR WORK IS FINISHED; GET OUT in the NAME OF JESUS, GET OUT, OUT!

Forms and sicknesses commonly caused by Witchcraft.

The most common is the one they use to make you fall in love. Usually, it is placed on a wife, friend, girlfriend, etc. Another is used to destroy businesses or families so that the husband will leave his wife for someone else, So that they lose sexual function or for sickness. Ultimately, they make curses for anything you can imagine, and the saddest part is that these demons can stay in the family for generation until someone with the power of Christ comes and calls them out in the Name of Jesus.

Important! Due to the importance of this topic we expand on this issue in the book **'Freedom from Witchcraft.'**

MESSAGES TO REMEMBER

- *I have met many people that have been cursed.*
- *Approximately 98% of all people of Christ who have been freed through this ministry of deliverance had been cursed.*
- *All Curses or spells can be removed and broken through Jesus Christ.*
- *For God, nothing is impossible and distance doesn't matter.*

13.
TESTIMONIES AND PROCESS OF DELIVERANCE

In this chapter, specially in the testimonies within your process, please, analyse the questions and the way how I talk to the demon, so you can become familiar with these questions, and you can use them when you need to fight the enemy or to help anyone to be free.

13.1. Free from chronic depression, panic's attacks, anger, hatred, asthma, and pain.

This testimony comes from María (her name was changed). This was one of the strongest and difficult deliverances I have done, because I was just starting with the ministry, and I knew nothing about this young woman. She came to me and the demon manifested immediately with ferocity. Taking control of her body, and to make matters worse, the demon didn't speak either Spanish or English, just in a weird dialect, it was an African demon and he didn't want to leave, even though I insisted. Thank God, who guided us and allowed the demon to write, we could know his legal right. Knowing this, she confessed, renounced and asked for forgiveness to our Lord, this way she was freed. The problem with this girl was, although she was Christian, she visited and asked a witch for help, she and her boyfriend. Glory to Jesus Christ for his great love and power to free us from any force of the enemy.

THIS IS HER TESTIMONY:

Hello, my name is María, it is August, around 5 in the afternoon, I'm very glad because it has been around 3 weeks after my deliverance and here I am, giving you my testimony:

Before my deliverance, I was disoriented, lost, without any hope and FAITH. I didn't know what hope, FAITH, love or peace within my heart meant, or perhaps, I did know what they meant when I was a little girl. But when I grew up, there had been a long time since I felt peace in my home, with my family, with anybody or anything at all.

Now I have a lot of peace within me, I'm not longer afraid of the dark, but of the night, to those weird things that happened to me before, that I know a lot of people was suffering as well. I used to think that it was only me, but now that I opened my eyes and I searched for help, I know there are a lot of people like me that have been freed in the name of Jesus Chris. They feel the same peace as me. Well, I'm going to tell you how I was before, because I'm not longer like that.

> **Pastor:** Interesting, because you are Christian, a Christian woman who loves God. And yet, you had those problems, didn't you?
>
> **María**: Yes
>
> **Pastor:** How did you decide to ask for help? Who told you to search for help?
>
> **Maria:** Well, a normal day like any other, I was crying because I was depressed, those were my days back then;

I spent them crying, it was awful. To be honest, I spent almost the 24 hours of the days crying. If I was awake, I spent three of five hours crying, that was my life back then. One day a friend came to my workplace. He knew the Lord, and he came to my work and with any triviality thing he said to me I faded, I started to cry, and well... that touched his heart, he hugged me and with that he helped me a lot. And well, from there, he started to take me to self-improvement's group, but I found more help in the Lord, I took refuge in God. He helped me a lot by being my side to cheer me up, but those were just runaways of my reality, then he suddenly asked me, what's the matter, woman? I had taken my frustrations out on him, I went to groups, and activities and nothing filled my heart.

María: Nothing complimented me. He was desperate for seeing me this bad; one day I was fine, and another I was bad, another I was fine and so I spent those days, which were my life, full of fears, worries, I was afraid to be fine. After the deliverance I felt great, but weird, it was because I didn't feel peace for a long time, I didn't feel fine with myself for a long time, after that I went to a wonderful Christian camp.

Pastor: María, talking to the point about the deliverance, How many demons did God release you from?

María: From six, I had a demon for a long time, but we couldn't understand him because he wasn't able to speak Spanish.

Pastor: Yes, it was a demon who did not speak Spanish or English, it was African language, he was African, and I said this because I was there with you and the demon couldn't express to us, he couldn't write or express in our language, we even made him write but he wrote a strange name. The important thing here is that our lord Jesus Christ deliverances María; now María is a new woman in the Lord.

María: Yes, as God says, and God wants us, from joy to joy.

María: Although we are Christians, there will be problems, but at least we know how to deal with them, how to say to any demonic attack that they have nothing to do with us, that they have to go away, we can do it with the Word of God and we can be free.

Pastor: In your case, what do you recommend us as a young woman? What do you suggest to the people around your age, younger or older than you? If they feel something strange in their body or their behavior, that isn't normal, if they feel that there is something supernatural within them that can do anything to affect them negatively, what would you tell them? Would you encourage them to search for help? To do a deliverance? What would you tell them?

María: Of course I would, I encourage them to search for people who have knowledge about deliverances and want to be free, we have to go to the Church, yes, we do, but this save you from a lot of years of sufferings, it saves you from years of feeling bad, this deliverances you. For me it took around two hours, this releases you in one day, this is unbelievable, what you have lived for lots of years, they take it away in just one day... it's wonderful, it's beautiful because I know that from now on my life have changed, it will keep changing and it will keep bringing me beautiful and enjoyment things and everything will be fine. I won't suffer anymore...NO, I do everything focused on Christ.

Pastor: Ok, thank you very much, María, what we are doing here is to expand God's kingdom, do you allow us to put this video on YouTube? So other people can benefit with this testimony, that the power of God, the power of JESUS CHRIST is tremendous, it's powerful, but there are also demons that torment us, even within Christians, Ok? Do you allow us to put this video on YouTube?

María: Yes, of course, I want to share something more with you. I didn't smile before, I was very active when I was little girl, in other words I spent all day doing good things, I was very cheerful, everything was positivism, and then I became the exact opposite, I was super negative, I said "but" to everything, a no; all was a no, no thank you and stuff like that. Now, even if I driving, I do it with a smile on my face, it's amazing what happened to me.

Pastor: Glory to JESUS CHRIST, all the honor. God bless you, María, all the honor and Glory to Our Lord Jesus Christ. Amen.

13.2. The process of deliverance from the "La Peau de Chagrin" agreement.

Analyze this process.

Satan uses any method to destroy the human being, and the media is not an exception, among these are the television, novels, etc. In this deliverance, we can see clearly how a person is released from a demon from an agreement or phrase that was on the novel "La Peau de Chagrim" or "The Wild Ass's Skin". I clarify that I have never saw it or heard about it. This person, being a child, saw it and repeated the agreement on his innocence, from that moment, the demon entered his body using this agreement.

In this case, the demon manifested talking to us; **this is the process of deliverance.**

> **Roger:** Demon, what's your name?
>
> **Demon:** Leave me alone.
>
> **Roger:** What's your name?
>
> **Demon:** Leave me alone.
>
> **Roger:** Do you have legal right to be here?
>
> **Demon:** Yes.
>
> **Roger:** Which one?
>
> **Demon:** He made an agreement.
>
> **Roger:** What agreement?
>
> **Demon:** He made an agreement.
>
> **Roger:** Which one?
>
> **Demon:** The one from the Wild Ass's Skin.
>
> **Roger:** Explain yourself!
>
> **Demon:** He read the story of The Wild Ass's Skin where agreements with the devil are made. He made the same agreement, he didn't know what he was doing, the same agreement from the novel of The Wild Ass's Skin, he made it, and you won't break it, hahaha (laughs).

Roger: What did he ask for?

Demon: He asked for everything, everything, things... everything, everything, everything, he was a kid; he was a catholic kid... HAHAHA (laughs).

Roger: What you have said, can you support it to the throne of the Lord God?

Demon: Of course I can. It's true, it's true. He knows it, he knows it.

Roger: You are right, if you are here is because you are right, an agreement is an agreement, that's your legal right.

Demon: Then, why do you ask? Leave me alone, I'm going back to my hole.

Roger: No, you are not. In the name of Jesus, not yet. How are you hurting him?

Demon: I'm not hurting him; I'm the one that gave him everything.

Roger: An agreement is an agreement and you are fulfilling it, these are to be fulfilled. You are here to fulfill it.

Demon: Yes, I gave him everything, he is smart, HAHAHA.

Roger: Oh right, Wild ass's skin, in the name of Jesus, you are going away, I'm going to talk with Pedro. I call the human spirit of Pedro, go out.

Demon: I'm going back to my hole.

Roger: Yes, go. Pedro, did you hear what the demon said?

Pedro: Yes, I did. But I was a kid; I didn't remember anything, it was just a novel.

Roger: Ask for forgiveness to God in the Name of Jesus for this agreement and renounce to that. Tell the demon that the blood's agreement that Jesus made at the Calvary's Cross is enough to nullify the agreement.

Pedro: (He confessed)

Roger: Demon, did you hear that?

Demon: Is that easy, ah? Ah?

Roger: An agreement is an agreement, these are to be fulfilled, my Lord Jesus Christ, his agreement nullify yours, that is my Lord. Did you hear me?

Demon: Yes, I did.

Roger: Do you have any legal right to be here?

Demon: Yes, I do.

Roger: Do you?

Demon: No, I don't.

Roger: That's right, you don't have any legal right to be here, your agreement is nullified, get out immediately and go to the abysm in the Name of Jesus. Never again you will come back to this man. Get out! Get out! Glory to Jesus Christ, you are free!

13.3. Process of deliverance from the demon of the Death Saint

This deliverance was done Online at our headquarters from USA to Mexico. This time, a young woman named Ana (changed name), she suffered from fear, horror, anxiety and madness. She went many times to hospitals and even tried to commit suicide by cutting her wrists more than seven times. After expelling many demons, the last one stayed and was reluctant to go; we found out that she made an agreement with that demon known in Mexico as the Saint Death, which millions of Mexicans worship, even with procession and all. This is the process of deliverance. Thank to our Lord Jesus Christ that we always found victory in him; we give all the honor and glory just to him.

This is the Process of Deliverance

> **Pastor:** Did she make an agreement with you?
>
> **Demon:** Yes, she did.
>
> **Pastor:** What agreement did she do?
>
> **Pastor:** Did she make an agreement with you?
>
> **Demon:** She would always ask me, in every moment. She promised me that when her son grows up, he would do the same as well, and that's why she is mine.
>
> **Pastor:** Are you the demon of the Death Saint?
>
> **Demon:** Yes, I am. She is mine. Do you understand?
>
> **Pastor:** I'm listening to you, I'm listening to you, I understand the agreement, I know agreements are to be

fulfilled, she committed a big sin, I understand that perfectly, the agreements are to be fulfilled, I get it. What you are saying, can you support it on the throne of the Lord as a truth?

Demon: That's right.

Pastor: Ok then, now I'm going to talk with this little girl. You are leaving for now in the name of Jesus, I'm going to talk with her.

Pastor: What the demon says, is it true?

Ana: What?

Pastor: What the demon says, is it true? About making an agreement, did you give your son?

Ana: Yes, I did.

Pastor: What did you give in the agreement? What did you give him or what happened?

Ana: I asked Death Saint before my son was born. I was told that I *couldn't get pregnant, so I prayed Saint Death and two weeks later I knew that I was pregnant, then I promised her that my son would herding it as well.*

Pastor: When was that?

Ana: 8 years ago.

Pastor: You didn't know anything about Jesus Christ? You didn't know the Word of God?

Ana: No, I carried a little chain with the image of Death Saint

Pastor: Ok, I'm recording all this. Some people are erroneous, my God, there are a lot of people that are erroneous, they are confused, and they are... what an error in Mexico, what an error, making agreements with demons, Death and those things.

Pastor: Was that the agreement with the Death Saint ? Those are problems.

Ana: Yes.

Pastor: Ok, close your eyes, you are now with the Lord, you are now with Christ as well. Close your eyes. In the Name of Jesus, I talk to the demon, Death Saint, you are there, go out from that darkness, will you kneel before the throne of the Lord God immediately? Are you there? Death, are you there?

Demon: Yes.

Pastor: Death, did you hear me? Do you still have the legal right before this woman? Answer in the Name of Jesus Christ. Death, were you there because of the agreement that this woman made? Agreements are to be fulfilled, right?

Demon: That's right.

Pastor: But did you hear this woman? This woman was forgiven, that agreement she made with you; you know that is nullified, don't you? Do you understand? You are a high rank demon from Mexico being acting heavily. Yo must know very well the Word of god, actually, it isn't your fault, it's the fault of the person, people committing sins doing things that they shouldn't do, against the Word of God, what you do is to fulfill the sin. Killing, stealing, destroying, people are the problems, the same people committing sins. You are a high Rank demon from Mexico, aren't you?

Demon: Yes, I am.

Pastor: Do you have many people who follow you in Mexico?

Demon: A lot.

Pastor: To the people, what do you have to say? Something in favor of Christ. What do you want to say to the people? I'm recording you, demon of the Death. What would you say to humanity?

Demon: Jesus is the way.

Pastor: What else?

Demon: If they believe in their God, why do they search for me?

Pastor: That's right.

Demon: Why do they search for me?

Pastor: That's right, that's a good question.

Pastor: It's the people, it's the sin; it's the ignorance of the people, it's the sin; it's the ignorance of the entire world.

Pastor: That's right, to do evil.

Demon: That's right.

Pastor: What a shame with Jesus Christ. Is there anything more that you want to say to the people, Death Saint ? Before you go.

Demon: Yes.

Demon: That they don't play with me. Don't play with me.

Pastor: What else? Were you explicit with the people?

Demon: They searched for me only to fulfill little whims, it doesn't work like that.

Pastor: For example, what did the people from Mexico ask for? What was the most common thing?

Demon: They asks me to bring back a person or to be successful in a business. Or a dirty business. But I am very jealous, I want them to worship anyone but me, and no other god.

Pastor: That's right; do you have any more demons inside this woman? Do you have any more demons inside them?

Demon: Suicide, ruin, familiar problems, diseases, they are what I have inside her.

Pastor: And the son?

Demon: He will suffer the same fate as his mother.

Pastor: Oh right, demon of the Death. First, all the demons in your kingdom have to leave, either in this woman and in the child, immediately, in the Name of

Jesus, get out immediately. For now, you stay, demon of the Death.

Pastor: You stay there, in the Name of Jesus, set her free, and her child too, in the Name of Jesus Christ, my Lord. Did they already obey, Death? Is there any demon from your kingdom, Death? Death, are they all gone? In the name of Jesus answer me yes or no, Death, are you listening to me?

Demon: Just a few.

Pastor: Make them go away in the Name of Jesus; are you alone in there, Death?

Demon: We are a few.

Pastor: Ok, in your kingdom, are they all gone? Or there is anyone else in your kingdom?

Demon: Not anymore.

Pastor: Ok. Either in this woman and the child, there aren't any more demons in your kingdom, are there?

Demon: No, there aren't (moving the head).

Pastor: There aren't more, can you support it before the throne of the Lord?

Demon: Yes, I can (moving the head).

Pastor: Ok, demon of the Death, Is there any other kingdom next to yours? Are there several leaders in there, any strong demon? Or are you alone?

Demon: I am alone.

Pastor: Can you support this before the throne of the Lord, what you say is the truth?

Demon: Yes, I can (moving the head).

Pastor: Ok, before this, in the name of Jesus, I command you to suggest the way that we have to follow, the way of Jesus Christ, oh right?

Demon: Yes.

Pastor: They can only search for Jesus Christ, to my Lord, he is the way. Ok, demon of the death, are you ready to go away, Death? Are you ready to let this woman and her family alone? Ok, get out from there in the Name of Jesus forever, in the Name of Jesus, the nightmare of this woman is ended, she is free forever. Now she is free, Ana, you are free in the name of Jesus Christ, it shouldn't be anything in there, ok? Is there any demon associated with Ana in there? Ok. Relax, Ana. There... I'm just talking to Ana. How are you?

Ana: I feel relaxed, I was nervous, but I am a bit better now.

Pastor: Give thanks to Jesus Christ, but only to Christ, sister.

Ana: That's right.

Pastor: Give thanks to him!

Pastor: Give thanks to Jesus Christ... repeat after me. I am his.

Pastor: The blood of Jesus bought me.

> **Ana:** The blood of Jesus bought me.
>
> **Pastor:** Give thanks to Jesus Christ because he deliverances you.
>
> **Ana:** Thank my God for having me freed.
>
> **Pastor:** Say it, thanks to Jesus Christ.
>
> **Ana:** Thanks to Jesus Christ, thank you because I am free, because from now on I am a different woman, because I am a new creature. Thank you because you forgave all my sins, you nullify that agreement that I had with the Death Saint, and in the same way, you took my son's curse, that Curse before he was born, thank you Father, I trust you, Lord, thank you, Lord Jesus.

13.4. Testimony and process of deliverance from Type 2 Diabetes

There are millions of people that are suffering from diabetes; it is a very common disease; that is why we put it in this book.

Note: Due to this disease from diabetes being one of the most popular in this century, we have decided to put it on our next book **FREEDOM FROM DISEASES** with its respective process of healing; for this time, study this short process of deliverance, and how to remove that demon from Diabetes.

PROCESS AND TESTIMONY OF DELIVERANCE– DIABETES

> **Pastor:** Today is September 9th, 2014, Brother, why do you require the deliverance?

Pedro: I have diabetes, I'm 24 years old, and my whole family from my dad side is diabetic. I have a son, and the true is I would want to enjoy life with him, but in the rock named Jesus Christ. I see a lot of pastors who have diabetes, then I say, they are pastors, they worship God and they say to me that God healed them by faith. In other words, we can't see it, I'm not skeptical, I just think different, I have a different idea about that. If God heals you, it's because the diabetes was gone, and though, they keep saying, for example, oh, my diabetes! And they embraced their disease. I want to be healthy from diabetes; my mom is leader of intersession and she couldn't heal me, yet, she could heal a lot of people, except me, and she has diabetes too. I'm worried about her, I want to enjoy life with her as well. My dad died in 2009 and the true is I would want to enjoy life with her as much as possible, but now I don't earn lots of money. I mean, I spent it almost all in debts. I can say I earn one thousand Mexican pesos, I keep to myself around one hundred or fifty five Mexican pesos for the week, and I go on and on like that as we say vulgarly here. I want to change my vocabulary, I want to be a good person, responsible, do the God's work. However, does God allow me to do it? And the true is I want to be different, I want to testify that diabetes has a cure and its name is Jesus Christ.

Pastor: Amen, amen. With that introduction of yours, almost complete, thank the Lord; we are going to your deliverance, Brother. It's September 9th of 2014 in Seattle, Washington in the United States; my Brother is in Cancun, Mexico, using the Internet as a technology for the glory of Jesus Christ.

To all the demons that are in this man, I talk to them in the Name of Jesus, especially to the highest Rank. To the most powerful demon, I command you to go out from the darkness, from that hole, and kneel before the throne of the Lord god. Demon, are you there?

Demon: Yes, I am.

Pastor: Are you there for the sin he committed? Was that the door? That's why you are inside this man. You have come to steal, kill and destroy, that's your nature, but it was for the sin, he offended the Lord, because holy is the Lord, holy, holy, that's right. Since when are you inside this man?

Demons: Since he was a kid, he was fifteen years old.

Pastor: And what did happen in the life of this man when he was fifteen years old?

Demons: He watched pornography.

Pastor: This man made a mistake, he made a mistake. How many demons do you have in your kingdom? In the name of Jesus, how many do you have?

Demons: 163

Pastor: Are you telling the true in front of the throne of the Lord?

Demons: No, hahaha (laughs).

Pastor: Speak the truth in the name of Jesus.

Demons: We are 8 powerful demons and we aren't going anywhere.

Pastor: You swear that you are 8 before the throne of the Lord?

Pastor: Demon, are you the chief in there?

Demons: Yes. I'm diabetes, laughs.

Pastor: Do you want to share a message about diabetes to the entire world and how do you get inside a body?

Demons: We work for it and we get inside through the gluttony, when they are not guarding God's temple, do you understand me? Pastors, normal people open doors there, and I'm not leaving him.

Pastor: Ok, you have many demons in this man. And in his family, how many do you have?

Demon: About six.

Consideration

Reader, you can realize that there are always leaders with several kingdoms.

Luke 8

[30] And Jesus asked him, what is your name? And he said: Legion; for many demons had entered him.

[31] They were imploring Him not to command them to go away into the abyss.

Pastor: Can you support what you say is the truth before the throne of the Lord?

Demon: Yes, I can.

Pastor: Diabetes, what other damage have you done to this man?

Demon: He can't be back with God. He can fornicate, and his lust will be strong, I convinced him easily, we dedicate to oppress.

Pastor: Is that your job? But the door, is it the sin?

Demon: Yes, it does.

Pastor: Because he offended the Holy, because holy he is, holy, holy. Is your name Diabetes?

Demon: I am the most famous and well-known spirit, I destroy and you can't get me out.

Pastor: You are one of the most well-known demons of the entire world.

Demon: And I am strong.

Pastor: Diabetes, you are a strong demon; then do you know the Word of God? Do you know that Jesus Christ paid with his blood for this man?

Demon: Yes, I do. But he made a sin, I have right over him, so I'm not going anywhere.

Pastor: Listen to me, it looks like that you didn't understand me, this man asked for forgiveness to God, and he does that, his sin is forgiven. The Lord forgave him, you were there for the sin, it's gone now; it disappeared, so your job is over. Jesus already paid for this man. Diabetes, tell your demon that they have to go away, always, in the name of Jesus.

Pastor: Are they gone? Diabetes, how many are left?

Demon: Six remain.

Pastor: Jesus shed his blood. Did he do it or not?

Demon: Yes, yes, he did. I was there.

Pastor: Ok, then, the six demons that remains there, they have to go in the Name of Jesus, forever.

Pastor: Diabetes, are you alone in there?

Demon: No, I'm not.

Pastor: Can you support it before the throne of the Lord?

Demon: Yes, I can.

Pastor: Get out from this man right now, one and for all.

Demon: No, no (groaning).

Pastor: You are free, brother!

Pastor: Open your eyes, Brother.

Pastor: How are you, Brother?

Pedro: I don't know, but my whole body shivered terribly.

Pastor: Give thanks to Jesus, Brother.

Pedro: Thank you, Jesus, thank you, Christ lives, Brother, he is so wonderful, I thought I was lost, I didn't believe in what you do, it isn't witchcraft or anything alike, I feel so good, so light, I feel like I was bathed like a baby (laughs). I give thanks to my lord Jesus, he deliveranced me. To be honest I was skeptical, Thank God for you; At the Churches, they are blinded, they cannot deliverance for themselves, they are not going the right way, the presence of God is at the Church, but there are also sick pastors, they need to do a deliverance.

"Now, we continue with the same deliverance, but it shows another demonic kingdom called **witchcraft.**"

Pastor: Brother, close your eyes, lift your head in the Name of Jesus, don't worry, you don't worry. I call the demon of Death Saint , are you there?

Pastor: Who are you in the name of Jesus? Are you here for the sin he committed?

Demon: Yes, I am.

Pastor: What sin it was? Witchcraft?

Demon: Yes.

Pastor: How did you get in this man, it was for food, or what?

Demon: No.

Pastor: Someone made a doll of this man.

Demon: Yes.

Pastor: Do you know that your time is over? Do you have to tell something to the people before you go?

Pastor: Oh right, don't leave anything in this man, no diseases, neither he or his family, neither his job, in the Name of Jesus, go away forever, this man is now free, go away forever. I nullify in the Name of Jesus any witchcraft, any spell, any prayer, any Word from the curse this man have received through dolls, pictures, food or drink, now I nullify all.

Pastor: Can you support it before the throne of the Lord?

Demon: Yes.**Pastor**: get out of this man for once and for always..

Demonio: no, no (gemidos).

Familiar: Brother, do you want to turn off the computer?

Pastor: I command you in the name of Jesus not to turn off the computer, I command you in the name of Jesus, your work is over in this man, get out of there, you have no legal right in this man.

Pastor: Why did you turn off the monitor?

Demon: I don't want to go, I disagree and I am not going anywhere.

Pastor: You know that holy is the Lord, holy, holy, don't you?

Demon: Shut up already, you are burning me. I am witchcraft; you don't remember me, do you? I'm gorgeous.

Pastor: Turn on the digital camera in the name of Jesus.

Pastor: We are under the throne of the Lord, the Supreme. Witchcraft, you are there because someone sent you through a doll, what did they do with the doll? Say it in the name of Jesus; did they put ties, needles, bindings? You know, this man belongs to Jesus Christ, the only way you will get out is breaking those bindings, and that's what I'm going to do now, Jesus Christ paid a price of Blood, he sent the God's sword where that doll is buried and with the tip of the sword he took away all the bindings, chains, ties, needles, from the head, and from the body. He nullifies all the spells, prayers and all the demonic work.

Pastor: I nullify it all, in the Name of Jesus, I clean him totally, I break every relationship from that doll with this man. There is a simple doll now and with the tip of the sword I break that doll, I destroy it completely. It's done, demon, go away in the name of Jesus, get out of there, this man is free, get out.

Pastor: Say I belong to Jesus Christ.

Pedro: I belong to Jesus Christ, the blood of Jesus bought me, thank you Jesus for having me deliveranced. Amen.

Pastor: You are free!

Pedro: Amen. Brother, I wanted to talk, but I couldn't, when I wanted to turn off the computer, I wanted to prevent it, but he didn't let me, he was oppressing, I only know that God deliverances me. Before praying, I felt a strong pain in my back, like two holes, it hurt pretty much. Now, I'm feeling the peace of Jesus Christ.**Pastor:** The sin is real, witchcraft is real, and it's tremendous.

Pedro: Yes, I've never felt this before, they always prayed for me, but I don't know what happened to me, my flesh moved, I was conscious but they didn't let me talk, that's how I felt, I d, but it was the other who obeyed.

Pastor: It's a reality, it's a reality.

Pastor: Demon from the ruin, are you there? In the Name of Jesus, who is there?

Pastor: In the name of Jesus, who are you, demon? Demon from the ruin, you are a demon very occupied in the entire world. Do you have anything to say to the people on ruin? Ruin, are you there for the sins of this man? He suffers the consequences because God is Holy, demon, do you know that this man was forgiven in the Name of Christ? Then go away and take every debt with you, in the Name of Jesus Christ. And the demons you have put in his family, creditors, and if one owed you money, it's going back in the Name of Jesus, is it clear? Every one of you, get out from the life of this man, free of debts, Jesus bought the life of this man with his own blood, everyone go away and the blood of Jesus Christ is enough, everyone get out from his pockets, from his wallet, wherever you are hiding, demon, this man is free, get out of there in the Name of Jesus from Nazareth.

Pedro: I feel less weight over my shoulders, I even felt my feet numb, now I feel my movement, I feel them lighter, and my headache is disappearing.

Pastor: Close your eyes, Brother, now you all, demons, when I say all of you, it's everyone including the generational demons, dislodge this man forever, from him, from his wife, kids, forever, is it clear? Immediately, in the name of Jesus Christ, get out from this man, and you take with you all the diseases, all, in the name of Jesus Christ. The one of the fornication as well, sexual aberration, adultery, lie, joke, all of them; this man has been forgiven, all the Curses he had for the sins he committed, from the sins of his ancestors, grandfathers, fathers, they are all nullified, because it's written. Cursed is everyone who is hung on a pole, Jesus Christ, my Lord. He became a Curse to take out all the Curses in his body. This man and all the humanity can be free for him, so go away, every one of you. Get out from his eyes, his head, his ears, his understanding, dislodge him in the name of Jesus, his back, Jesus forgave him, he paid a price for him, it was his Holy Blood, He rescued him from the darkness to his kingdom of light. You, demons, have nothing to do now, this man is a new creature, dislodge him from his back, his head, his heart, this man is a son of God. Loneliness, depression, Saint Death, disease, you are going away forever in the Name of Jesus, from their private parts as well, from his stomach, hands, feet, in the name of Jesus, get out of this man, I destroy all the chains that stood in the way to prevent this man to move forward, in the Name of Jesus Christ.

Pastor: I destroy it all, all the ties. In the name of Jesus, this man is free for the blood of Jesus Christ, he's been bathed, this man is totally free, his wife, his sons, daughters, this man is free because Jesus paid at the Calgary's Cross for the Price of his sins, this man was guilty, he had to pay, for that reason Jesus paid in his place at the Cross, they beat him, they crucified him, he was insulted, he was pierced, he shed his blood, all his debts is totally nullified, Jesus died and resurrected, and he is seated next to our Father God.

This man is free, he is free, all of you go away, forever, immediately. The debt was paid with the blood Jesus shed, so all of you in the name of Jesus, go away now, nothing unclean stay, this man has been sanctified and justified, he's been redeemed, he's been rescued, so everyone of you are uprooted in the name of Jesus, out and forever, get out, all of you, demons, you are nullified, your job in this man is over. The blessing of Jesus Christ is in this man.

Brother, YOU ARE FREE AND HEALTHY!

-Amen, glory to God, THANK YOU, JESUS!

13.5. Testimony of health: Chronic diseases such as diabetes, thyroids, anger, high blood pressure and rosacea.

Testimony of Fidelina Umbert from Argentina...

I asked for help because despite having received Christ within my heart as a Savior and Lord, I had outburst of anger, wrath and fights at moments. I didn't know why. I also suffered from chronic diseases such as diabetes, thyroids, high blood pressure and rosacea (skin condition causing redness, especially in the face). Every day my face was worse.

That's why I asked Pastor Roger for help. He decided to do a prayer of deliverance, where I manifested with a lot of demon. It was hardworking; the Pastor was fighting with the legion of demons around two hours. These demons took control of my body and my mind. They brought all these diseases to my body. But thanks to the deliverance by the pastor, in the Name of Jesus, I have no longer have outburst of anger and I am free. My diseases are well controlled, I stopped taking pills and the rosacea from my face disappeared completely. My face has no marks, everything disappeared and didn't come back in the Name of Jesus. With this, we realized that Christians can have demons like I did. They cause you diseases and all kind of problems for your life. I thank Pastor Roger D Muñoz for letting himself be guided and used by our Lord Jesus Christ. I bless him in the Name of Jesus alongside the minister Cristo Libera.

13.6. Testimony of Curse words

We must be very careful with words we say or others say to us.

> - I remember one woman I was ministering who couldn't get pregnant. In the deliverance; the demon manifested and confessed he was called Infertility. He had entered the day her mother in law yelled at her that she would never get pregnant again. Actually, she never could have more children.

> - I was once ministering a Pastor who wasn't doing good in his job. The demon manifested and confessed he had the guilt of the failure of the Pastor and he had entered since he was a child through his mother because she always said to him "You have butterfingers, everything you touch, you destroy it". And for that reason, the demon of destruction

entered his body, thanks to Jesus he released him and his life changed.

- On another ministration, a demon manifested who didn't want to go, and he answered me with fury. *HOW DO YOU WANT ME TO GO AWAY? DON'T YOU SEE THAT SHE SWORE AND SAID DAMN YOU A THOUSAND TIMES OVER, DO YOU? HOW DO YOU WANT ME TO GO?*

- Many people wish to die, and demons of death enter their bodies, this is very common.

14.
FORMULARY QUESTIONS

Important information before completing this form

This is the key part of this Book, please fill out the form with all diligence and sincerity, and please, fast at least three days before deliverance.

The goal of completing this form is to find the possible doorways of demons and diseases. Therefore, be honest and thorough in your responses as it will make it easier for your deliverance and healing.

James 5:16 *(KJV)*

16 Confess your faults one to another, and pray one for another, that ye may be healed.

Fill the release form. These are questions that are made to seek out possible doorways for demonic access.

Matthew 6:14-15 *(KJV)*

14 For if ye forgive men their trespasses, your heavenly Father will also forgive you:

¹⁵ But if ye forgive not men their trespasses, neither will your Father forgive your trespasses.

In Jesus Christ, we are redeemed from the curse of the law, the iniquities of our sins and those of our ancestors, Gal 3:13. However, the demons do not leave; they are left without legal right in our bodies and our family, resulting in sickness and suffering. They make it possible, so the key is to try to seek out our sins and those of our ancestors, to identify them, give them up so that we can cast the demons quickly and thus eradicate our family curses of diabetes, cancer, alcoholism, poverty.

NOTE: This form is in letter size, largest in our Book Manual deliverance to facilitate the printing, along with more important prayers

FORMULARY QUESTIONS

Date: _____

Full Name:
_____

Country, City, Neighborhood or Colony:
_____

Telephone: _____

E-mail:_____

Age: _____

Single ( ) Married ( ) Widowed ( ) Divorced ( ) Attached ( ) Couple / Groom ( )

How often: _____ Explain:
_____
_____

Profession:
_____

Principal occupation or job function:
_____

What is your background in the church with Jesus Christ?
_____

Did you accept Jesus as your Lord and Savior? ( ) Christian Evangelical -Protestant- ( ) Since when?
_____
_____

Already baptized? At what age approximately._____

Were you baptized in the Name of the Father, Son, and Holy Spirit?

_____

_____

Decimates? _____

How many children do you have? ____ Are they believers? _____ Explain:

_____

_____

_____

_____

SECTION OF THE ANCESTORS AND ANCESTRY

Please investigate and calmly write everything you know or suspect of your ancestors, including your uncles, cousins, current and past family, because there may be Curses in our families that are caused by them which could be affecting everyone. In most of the deliverance conducted, I find demons that have been present since before birth. I repeat, Curses and sins through Jesus Christ have been removed, but the demons do not leave, they remain, and are responsible for those diseases.

Do you know if some of your ancestors, parents, grandparents, etc., have made pacts, practiced, participated or suffered from witchcraft, cleaning, bathrooms, good luck, adultery, fornication, divorce, drunkenness, sexual perversion, bestiality, alcoholism , disease, depression, mental disorders, diabetes, insanity, adultery, anger, criminal activities, births outside marriage, Satanism?

Write down everything that the Holy Spirit will bring to mind.

___

SECTION FROM CONCEPTION TO BIRTH

Try to find out everything.

How was your delivery? Was it by caesarean? Normal delivery? Explain:

___

When your mother was pregnant. Was she loved? Was it an occasional love? Was she married? Was your father aware? Was it by rape? Was he/she drunk etc.? What do you know? Explain:

___

Trauma, falls, accidents during pregnancy. Yes ( ) No ( ) Explain:

___

Was the pregnancy rejected? Was it unwanted? Was there an attempted abortion? Explain Curse words:

___

Were both parents Christians? Yes ( ) No ( ) Explain:

___

SECTION - FROM BIRTH TO ADOLESCENCE

Were you adopted? Yes ( ) No ( ) Explain:

_____
_____

Did you meet your parents? Yes ( ) No ( ) Explain:

_____
_____

How was your relationship with each of them? Explain:

_____

Were there fights and Curses at home? Yes ( ) No ( ) Explain:

_____
_____

Were you raised in a Christian home? Yes ( ) No ( ) Explain:

_____
_____

Curses spoken as: You're a lazy, good for nothing, you're a failure? Explain:

_____

Were phrases such as you have hands Lumber and destroy everything you touch used in your home.... etc.?

_____

Were you sexually abused? Yes ( ) No ( ) If Yes, Who abused you?

_____

Were you abused physically and / or psychologically? Physical ( ) Psychological ( ). Explain:

_____

Did you participate in sexual games like mom and dad ... Etc.?
Yes ( ) No ( ) Explain:

How was your childhood? Example: Loneliness, Rejection, Fights ... Etc.:

Was any of your ancestors, parents, grandparents, great-grandparents or yourself, involved in congregations like Jehovah's Witnesses, Unitarians, Mormon, Rosicrucians, New Age, Buddhism, Stop Suffering, Atheism, Christian Science, Mason, Satanism ... Etc.? Yes ( ) No ( ) Explain:

Do any of your ancestors, parents, grandparents, great-grandparents or yourself, have or have had any of the following illnesses: Schizophrenia, Madness, Fear, Nervousness, Anxiety, Mental disorders, Tumor, Cancer, Asthma, Diabetes ... etc.? Yes ( ) No ( ) Explain:

Have you seen movies of Terror, Fear, Violence, Death, Porn, Sex, Mocking, etc.?

What Video Games, Ouija . Etc. have you seen or played? You name them.

Magic games, Fighters, Murderess Explain:

SECTION FOR GENERAL QUESTIONS:

Are you proud?

_____

Have you watched pornography? Yes ( ) No ( ) Explain:

_____
_____
_____
_____

Do you Masturbate Yes ( ) No ( ):

_____

Have you seen or practiced sexual aberrations: Sex with animals, Homosexuality, Lesbianism, Prostitution, etc.? Yes ( ) No ( ) Explain:

_____
_____
_____
_____

Have you seen or practiced fornication? Yes ( ) No ( ) Explain:

_____

Are you/ were you an adulterer? Yes ( ) No ( ) Explain:

_____

Do you live with a partner, without being married? Yes ( ) No ( ) Explain: _____

These doors are very common tickets demons:

These questions are for you, your spouse, boyfriend or girlfriend, because each person brings with them demonic bondage from their past that also they could be affecting you, besides these questions apply to the present or past, Fill what you practiced in the past and present.

How many girlfriends (I), friends (you) have you had sex with? Explain

_____
_____

Do you know or suspect if any past or present family couple practice witchcraft?

_____
_____

How many times have you been divorced or separated?

_____
_____

Do you have or had enemies? Have you fought? Are you upset? Explain:

_____
_____

Are you envious? Explain:

_____
_____

Do you use Alcohol, Drugs, Cocaine, Marijuana ... Etc.?

_____
_____

Do you have tattoos on your body? Explain:

_____

Do you have any amulet for "protection" or "Good luck" ... Etc.?

_____
_____

Do you have or have had any image, objects of idolatry, Rosaries, Holy pictures of saints, or otherwise related to Catholicism? Are they on your neck, quarter, home, car, office ... Explain?

_____
_____

Have you been baptized before into "Sainthood" Example: Virgin del Carmen, San Gregorio ... Etc. Explain?

_____
_____

Why were you given your name? For example, you could not be born, and your mother prayed to San Pedro and therefore you are called Pedro.

_____
_____

Have you entered into witchcraft Covenants? Yes ( ) No ( ) Explain:

_____
_____

Do you know or suspect if anyone have made covenants with witchcraft for you or your ancestors? Yes ( ) No ( ) Explain:

_____
_____

Do you know what the previous tenants in your present apartment were involved in? Do you know what sins were practiced?

_____
_____

Did you pray or spiritually cleansed the home before moving in? Yes ( ) No ( ) Explain:

_____

Do you know of a nearby neighbor who practices occultism? Yes ( ) No ( ) Explain:

_____
_____

Did your problems begin since you moved to this new house? Yes ( ) No ( ) Explain:

_____
_____

Has there been Fights, taps, such heaviness, shortage ..., etc. Explain:

_____
_____

Do you feel strange noises at home? Yes ( ) No ( ) Explain:

_____
_____

Have you had any accidents or traumas? Examples: Robberies, Car crashes, Operations Etc. Yes ( ) No ( ) Explain:

_____
_____

What are your diseases, sufferings?

_____

_____

What medicines do you take?

_____

_____

Do you suffer from Fears, Depression, and Stress ... Etc.? Yes ( ) No ( ) Explain:

_____

_____

Have you lost any dear ones? Were they family members, friends? Their names and details.

_____

_____

Do you work/ have you worked in Funeral homes, hospitals or places related to death, blood, and pain? etc.?

_____

_____

Do you have any addiction? Yes ( ) No ( ) Explain:

_____

_____

Have you practiced Yoga, Karate or Martial Arts? Yes ( ) No ( ) Explain:

_____

_____

What kind of music did you listen to before becoming a Christian? Give details

_____

_____

Have you seen Horror movies, Violence, Magic, Batman ... Etc.?

_____
_____

Do you have nightmares? Are they repetitive? Almost the same? Give details

_____
_____

Do you like and watch boxing, wrestling, action movies? Give details and indicate the names of the main actors you admires

_____
_____

What is your hobby, passion? In which do you spend more leisure time?

_____
_____

Are you rebellious? Yes ( ) No ( ) Explain:

_____
_____

Do you have hatred? Yes ( ) No ( ) Explain:

_____

Have you forgiven and asked for forgiveness? Yes ( ) No ( ) Explain:

_____
_____

Have you Cursed Satan and his principalities, rulers ... etc.? Yes ( ) No ( ) Explain:

_____
_____

Have you been angry with God? Yes ( ) No ( ) Explain:

_____

_____

Make a list of all your sins not listed above. Employ a good time and ask the Holy Spirit to remind you. This is to know what could be hidden or demon to finally cast out.

_____

What do you think are the causes of your problem you think? In this section, write what you think is important for us to know that will contribute to your deliverance and healing.

_____
_____
_____
_____

REFLEXION

God chose Moses as the leader to free his people from slavery, and he **obeyed him**. Because he was with God's power.

God chose Joshua as the successor leader of Moses to conquer the Promised Land that was dominated by the enemy and he **obeyed him**.

God sent his loved Son Jesus Christ to free us from the slavery of Satan, and he **obeyed him**.

Jesus Christ chose his apostles to extend the kingdom of God with signs and wonders, freeing and healing with the power of the Holy Spirit and they **obeyed him**. Jesus Christ chose this Ministery of Deliverance CRISTO LIBERA to keep going freeing and healing his people, and we are **obeyed him**. This Minister of deliverance by order of our Lord Jesus Christ is giving you these books of Deliverance, the powerful weapons of the spiritual war that we are using successfully. **Now is your responsibility!**

The question is... What will you do?

1 Samuel 15:22b

²² To obey is better than sacrifice

2 Timothy 2:2 (RVR 1960)

And the things you heard me say in the presence of many witnesses, entrust to reliable people who will also be qualified to teach others.

Matthew 10:8 (RVR 1960)

⁸ Heal the sick, raise the dead, cleanse those who have leprosy drive out demons, freely you have received, freely give.

God in the name of Jesus and with his Holy Spirit give you wisdom and discernment to take the best decision of your life. BROTHERS AND SISTERS THE FIELDS ARE RIPE FOR HARVEST. ARE YOU WILLING TO HARVEST?

FINAL RECOMMENDATION

Implement all these Weapons Spiritual Warfare.
Evangelize with our series of Books Freedom.
Moreover, recommend our series.
Get Book Manual: Freedom.
Return to study this Book.

Roger D Muñoz

CHRIST LIBERA
MINISTRY OF DELIVERANCE AND HEALING
Seattle WA 98115

www.cristolibera.org

Get our Series of Freedom

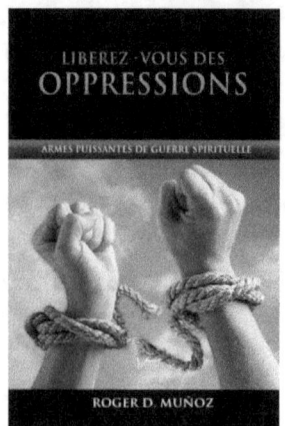
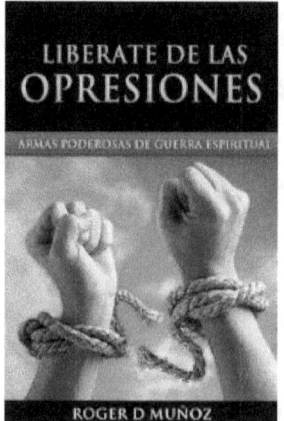

www.ingramcontent.com/pod-product-compliance
Lightning Source LLC
Chambersburg PA
CBHW071916290426
44110CB00013B/1374